High-Tech Babies

The Debate Over Assisted Reproductive Technology

ISSUES IN FOCUS TODAY

Kathleen Winkler

Enslow Publishers, Inc.
40 Industrial Road
Box 398
Berkeley Heights, NJ 07922
USA

http://www.enslow.com

Library of Congress Cataloging-in-Publication Data

Winkler, Kathleen.
    High-tech babies : the debate over assisted reproductive technology / Kathleen
Winkler.
        p. cm. — (Issues in focus today)
    Includes bibliographical references and index.
    ISBN 0-7660-2528-4
    1. Human reproductive technology—Juvenile literature. 2. Human reproductive
technology—Moral and ethical aspects—Juvenile literature. 3. Medical ethics—
Juvenile literature. 4. Health risk assessment —Juvenile literature. 5. Multiple
pregnancy—Juvenile literature. I. Title. II. Series.
    RG133.5.W546 2006
    618.1'78—dc22

                                                    2005034656

Printed in the United States of America

10 9 8 7 6 5 4 3 2 1

To Our Readers:
We have done our best to make sure that all Internet Addresses in this book were active
and appropriate when we went to press. However, the author and publisher have no control over and assume no liability for the material available on those Internet sites or on
other Web sites they may link to. Any comments or suggestions can be sent by e-mail to
comments@enslow.com or to the address on the back cover.

Illustration Credits: Courtesy of Dr. Brian Bear, p. 26; courtesy of Marilyn D. Benz, p. 57;
Getty Images, pp. 32, 89; courtesy of Dr. Yingli He, pp. 3, 29; courtesy of Huntington
Reproductive Center, p. 73; Coneyl Jay/Photo Researchers, Inc., pp. 3, 85; courtesy of
Dr. Rachel Mann, pp. 42, 51, 83; courtesy of Medical College of Wisconsin, pp. 3, 54;
courtesy of Nightlight Christian Adoptions, pp. 3, 60, 76; Photos.com, pp. 3, 5, 12, 16,
39, 63, 67, 71, 79, 81, 91, 93; Rubberball Productions, pp. 1, 19, 22, 46; courtesy of
Dr. Estril Strawn, p. 35; courtesy of Kathleen Winkler; used with permission, p. 10.

Cover Illustrations: Courtesy of Medical College of Wisconsin (background); Photos.com
(large photo); BananaStock (small photo).

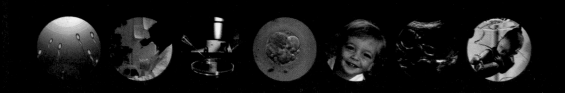

C o n t e n t s

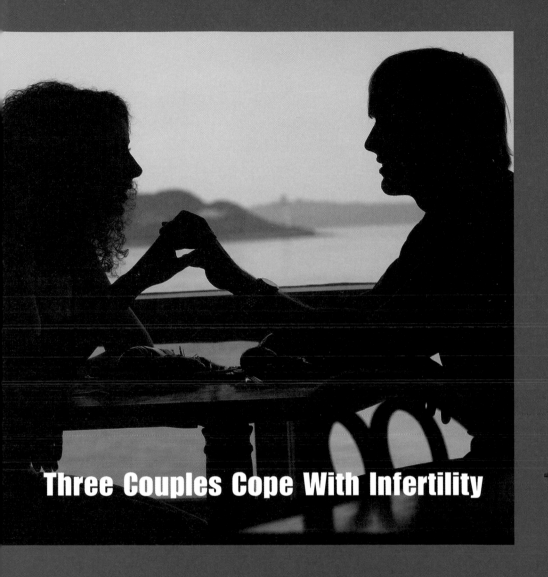

Three Couples Cope With Infertility

Infertility—the inability to become pregnant—hits many couples like an earthquake. All around them friends are blossoming with babies like flowers in the spring. They decide that their turn has come, throw out the contraceptives (if they have been using them), and wait to blossom themselves. And wait. And wait some more.

Wanting to become pregnant, wanting a baby more than anything else in the world, while your systems do not seem to be working, can be one of the most stressful situations a couple can face. It must seem, to them, trying to conceive and being disappointed each month, that life is completely unfair as they see pregnant woman everywhere. Yet pregnancy eludes them.

But there is hope for couples that are struggling with infertility. Specialists in the medical field called assisted reproductive technology (ART) are helping women become pregnant using a variety of different medical techniques. The field is new and changing very fast. Techniques that were cutting edge a few years ago have been expanded and improved, resulting in even better ones. Research is ongoing to find new methods to replace the ones used today.

Yet while these better techniques have made it possible for more couples to conceive and have a baby, there are many ethical questions about what they need to do to make that happen. Some people and organizations object to some of the techniques. Some religions, including Roman Catholicism, Orthodox Judaism, and some others, believe that creating a baby outside the "natural system" of intercourse between husband and wife is wrong. Others think that using eggs or sperm donated by someone else is unethical. Some people think only certain donations are unethical, such as using a brother or sister's sperm or eggs. Some people object to a couple using another woman to carry their baby—they ask whose baby it really is. All these issues will be discussed in a later chapter. First, meet three couples who are coping with infertility with different means and different outcomes.

Wanting to become pregnant while your systems do not seem to be working can be one of the most stressful situations a couple can face.

Joanna and Steve, Terry and Jim, and Lynn and Tim are all dealing with the pain of infertility. They all illustrate the ways medical science can work to improve the odds of pregnancy and, perhaps, give them the gift of a child.

Joanna and Steve

"Joanna" and "Steve" (not their real names) tried for a pregnancy for a year with no result.

"Trying" is a nonmedical term for having sexual intercourse without using contraceptives in an attempt to become pregnant. It may also include timing intercourse to be close to the point in the woman's cycle when an egg is released. (The scientific term for egg is *ovum.*)

After a year, Joanna and Steve went for an infertility workup, a series of tests to determine why she had not become pregnant.

"The workup found that Steve's semen had something in it which caused his sperm to swim poorly and clump together," Joanna explains. "We tried an intrauterine insemination." Steve's sperm was washed and concentrated and placed into Joanna's uterus through a tube called a cannula at the time of the month when her doctor could see she was going to release an egg. They tried this three times without success.

Next, Joanna took a fertility drug to make her ovaries produce more than the normal one egg a month. "It worked on the second try," Joanna said.

The result was wonderful—a baby girl, now almost three years old. But the procedure, while one of the least invasive that fertility doctors use, was still not easy. "Emotionally it is difficult because you have such high hopes every month and they are usually dashed," Joanna recalls. "But that did make the final result that much sweeter!"

Physically, a couple of the tests were somewhat painful, she says, and the drug she took to stimulate her ovaries made her feel moody and tense. But that did not stop Joanna and Steve from trying for a second baby. After five tries, this time without any fertility drugs, she has had her second baby girl.[1]

Terry and Jim

"Terry" and her husband, "Jim," had to go one step further than Joanna and Steve in their quest to have a baby. They used one of the most high-tech techniques: in vitro fertilization (IVF).

"We tried seriously for a couple of years," Terry says. "We didn't use any birth control and tried to time things, using ovulation kits. While we were doing all that, we still thought it was just going to happen. You know how people say, 'Just relax and you'll get pregnant?'"

They made their first appointment with an infertility specialist as Terry neared her thirtieth birthday. "I didn't want to be thirty without any kids," she says. "At that point, we wanted to know if something was medically wrong."

The couple had an infertility workup. It showed that Jim had a low sperm count and that one of Terry's tubes was slightly blocked. The fallopian tubes connect the ovaries (where the eggs are created) to the uterus (where the fertilized egg is implanted). If the tubes are blocked, the sperm cannot reach the egg. Knowing that, Jim and Terry thought the same procedure Joanna and Steve had used, intrauterine insemination (IUI), would be enough. But six IUIs didn't work, even with Terry taking a fertility drug.

At that point, they decided to try IVF, in which eggs and sperm are put in a dish where the sperm can fertilize the egg. The resulting embryos are transferred into the woman's uterus. Terry was given more powerful fertility drugs. Her eggs were removed while she was under general anesthetic, so she does not remember it. The eggs and Jim's sperm were mixed in a petri dish. On the first attempt, three eggs were fertilized. While the doctors did not think any of them were top grade (meaning very healthy), they transferred two to Terry's uterus. Unfortunately, it didn't work.

It was a hard decision to try IVF again, since it is very expensive and there are never any guarantees. But Terry and Jim decided on another try. This time it worked—two transferred embryos "took," and Terry was carrying twins.

Terry had a perfectly normal pregnancy. Her twins, a boy and a girl, are now three years old. Looking back, she says the procedures, which were not covered by insurance and cost nearly $10,000 each, took all their savings. "Luckily, we both had good jobs," she says. "I don't think we'd be able to do it now. But it really doesn't matter how much it cost. It was worth every penny."

Emotionally, the procedures were hard, Terry says. "Realizing that just because you've spent $10,000 doesn't mean you will have a baby is hard. It was rough when the first one didn't work. I cried for a day. But knowing that we could try again helped."[2]

It is not just the woman who can have a hard time with the emotional roller coaster. The husband has to deal with his own feelings and give his wife support at the same time. "We just tried to encourage each other that there was hope no matter what," Jim says.

Now that it is over, Jim loves his role as parent. He says, "Being a dad is just wonderful. I was talking to a friend whose wife is expecting twins. I told him it's just the best thing you can imagine—once they sleep through the night, that is! At age three they are just incredible."[3]

Lynn and Tom

Not every infertility story has a happy ending. For "Lynn" and "Tom," the story is not yet complete, but at this point, Lynn is not pregnant despite several ART procedures.

"We tried the old-fashioned way for about three years," she says. "We were starting a little bit late; I was thirty-six when we started trying." Because Lynn had endometriosis, a disorder of the lining of the uterus, they went right to ART.

Terry and Jim had twins, a girl and a boy, following two rounds of in vitro fertilization.

After several failed attempts at intrauterine insemination, they went to in vitro fertilization. Unfortunately, that didn't succeed either. The first try, three eggs were fertilized and transferred, but none became implanted.

Lynn became very depressed; her doctors put her on an antidepressant drug. "It's very common," Lynn says. "I'm still dealing with the depression."

Once she came off the antidepressant, she began to try again. One time she did produce a few eggs, but none of them were fertilized. After that, despite drugs that caused hot flashes and mood swings, she never produced any more eggs. "Finally I had to say, 'This is enough. I'm not going to put myself through this any longer.'"

That led her and Tom to the next step: using a donor. "We will try embryo donation," she says. In that procedure, "extra" embryos from another couple (which had been frozen) will be thawed and transferred into Lynn's uterus. "We went through an adoption agency in California that treats embryo donation as a normal adoption. We are in the process, we have been approved and I'm on estrogen [a hormone] to get my body ready to welcome a pregnancy. The doctors never make promises of course, but they think my chances are better with this."

If this doesn't work, Lynn and Tim will try to adopt a child. Just having that possibility gives Lynn hope. "Yesterday I saw a pregnant woman and for the first time I didn't burst into tears or feel resentful or angry at life," she says. "I was able to think, 'Well, good luck!'"

"When you jump through all these hoops, you want some guarantees," she adds. "And there aren't any guarantees. If this doesn't work, I will be devastated again, but I've always known that if the other steps . . . didn't work, we would adopt."[4]

Three couples. Three different approaches. Two happy endings; one as yet incomplete.

While there are no promises of success in the world of ART, there is much to be hopeful about. In this book, we will look closely at the medical procedures these couples used, and several more besides.

All of them have the same goal: a healthy baby.

2   # How Conception Happens

The female reproductive system is among the most complex in the human body. When you look at all the things that have to work perfectly for conception to take place, it is a wonder that any woman ever becomes pregnant. Yet, billions of human beings show that, indeed, it does happen!

To understand assisted reproduction, we first must understand two things: the normal female menstrual cycle, and then, how conception happens.

The Normal Menstrual Cycle

Looking at a newborn baby girl snuggled in her pink blanket, it is hard to imagine that she has all the equipment she will ever need to become a mother some day. But it is true. A baby girl is born with all the eggs she will ever use—and then some!—stored in her ovaries. That may be as many as four hundred thousand eggs, each one tucked into a nest of protective cells called a follicle.

As a girl reaches puberty—the age at which the human body first becomes capable of reproduction—her body will start making, all on its own, several different types of hormones. Hormones are chemical messengers that tell another part of the body to do something. They are needed for almost every bodily function, including digestion, growth, and reproduction. Some hormones have more than one function.

Think of the brain's pituitary gland as the conductor of an orchestra. Once a month, the conductor raises its baton and starts the symphony. Hormones from the brain tell the ovary to get ready to release an egg. The egg bursting out of its follicle is called ovulation. Since the open end of the fallopian tube, attached to the uterus, lies right next to the ovary, the egg is swept into the tube and starts its journey toward the uterus.

Meanwhile, back in the fallopian tube, the egg is traveling, moved along by tiny hairlike cells called cilia, toward the uterus. One of two things can happen. As the egg travels through the tube it may meet sperm from the woman's male partner swimming toward it. Or it may not.

Sperm is produced by the testicles and carried in a fluid called semen. Semen is projected into a woman's vagina during sexual intercourse. The man places his penis into

> A baby girl is born with all the eggs she will ever use—and then some!—stored in her ovaries. As many as 400,000 eggs are tucked into a nest of protective cells called a follicle.

How Birth Control Devices Work

Contraceptives—methods of preventing conception—generally work in one of three ways: by preventing the egg and sperm from coming in contact with each other, by preventing ovulation, or by preventing fertilization.

- Condoms: A condom is a tube of stretchy latex that looks something like a long, skinny balloon. It is placed over the penis to collect the sperm. There is also a female condom, a polyurethane sleeve inserted into the vagina to "line" it and collect the sperm.

- Diaphragm and cervical cap: The diaphragm is a rubber dome put into the vagina that covers the entrance to the uterus, called the cervix, to prevent sperm from entering. The cervical cap does the same thing, but it sits more snugly over the cervix. A doctor must fit both.

- Contraceptive sponge: A spongy material saturated with a chemical to kill sperm that is put into the vagina. It is sold without prescription.

- Spermicide: Foam or jelly containing a chemical that kills sperm. Spermicides are not very effective when used alone, but use with condoms increases the effectiveness of both. They are sold without prescription.

- Intrauterine device (IUD): A small, soft plastic object placed into the uterus by a doctor. Some contain a drug. According to the Web site of Planned Parenthood, "IUDs usually work by preventing fertilization of an egg. They seem to do it by affecting the way the sperm or eggs move. They also affect the lining of the uterus, which, in theory, may prevent implantation of a fertilized egg."[1]

- Birth control pills: Some pills contain a combination of two hormones, estrogen and progestin; they prevent ovulation by interrupting the normal

How Birth Control Devices Work *(continued)*

hormone cycle. They also thicken the mucus around the cervix so sperm cannot get through, and they change the lining of the fallopian tubes so an egg cannot move down them easily. Progestin-only pills, sometimes called minipills, do not contain estrogen. They are somewhat less effective than combined pills and must be taken at the same time every day.

- Shot, implant, and patch: Contraceptive hormones can be injected every three months. They can also be put in small, soft plastic capsules placed under the skin that are effective for five years, or put in a patch worn on the skin that must be changed periodically.

- Vaginal ring: A nickel-sized plastic ring inserted into the vagina that releases a contraceptive hormone.

- Emergency contraception (sometimes called the "morning-after pill," although that is not an accurate name): This pill contains a higher dose of the same hormones as in the combined pill. It must be taken within seventy-two hours of intercourse.

- Abstinence: Not having sexual intercourse. If there is no sperm, there can be no pregnancy.

- "Natural" contraception: Knowing when the woman is ovulating and avoiding intercourse at that time.

- Permanent contraception: Males can have a vasectomy, in which the tubes that carry sperm to the outside of the body are cut and sealed. A woman can have a tubal ligation, in which her fallopian tubes are cut and sealed. Sometimes these procedures can be reversed, but no one should count on that.[2]

the woman's vagina and ejaculates, or "squirts," the semen. Millions of sperm begin swimming toward the woman's uterus and fallopian tubes.

Suppose, however, there is no sperm to meet the egg. Perhaps the woman has not had sexual intercourse with a man. Or perhaps one of them is using a form of birth control that prevents the sperm and egg from meeting. In that case, the unfertilized egg simply passes into the uterus. Since the thick lining of the uterus is not needed, it begins to break down. It is shed from the woman's vagina; that is called menstruation, or a period. The cycle takes about twenty-eight days.

Birth control pills, first introduced in 1960, avert pregnancy by interrupting the normal hormone cycle and preventing ovulation.

How Conception Normally Happens

If sperm is present, egg and sperm can meet, usually in the fallopian tube. One sperm of the millions present in a normal male ejaculation penetrates the outer shell of the egg. The egg is fertilized; it can be said that conception has taken place.

At this point, the fertilized egg continues its journey to the uterus. There it normally finds a welcoming environment. If there are no problems, it attaches to the wall of the uterus, and the woman is pregnant. The fetus will develop and grow in the uterus for nine months ending with the birth of a baby.

While this all sounds very complicated—and it is—the process of conception makes sense if you look at it as a whole. The point of the entire thing is an attempt to reproduce, so the woman's body gets an egg ready to be fertilized and, at the same time, makes a safe place for it to attach and grow.

Usually, there is no way to tell what is happening inside a woman's body as this process plays out. Some women do feel a bit of pain in the lower abdomen when they ovulate. That may

Teen Myths About Conception

A survey done in England for a magazine called *Doctor* found that teens believe many myths about how conception happens and how to avoid it:

- Putting a watch around the penis prevents pregnancy because the radiation from the dial kills the sperm.

- Rinsing out the vagina with Coca-Cola prevents pregnancy.

- A man is fertile only if his testicles feel cold. (It is true, however, that high body temperature can kill sperm.)

- Pregnancy can be prevented by having the man drink a lot of alcohol.

- A woman can only get pregnant if she has sexual intercourse every night.

- Cellophane bags from snacks can be used as condoms.

None of these is true.[3]

be a clue that ovulation is happening, but it is not reliable enough to use alone as a guide to timing sexual intercourse either to cause or to prevent pregnancy.[4]

Now that we have seen how normal conception happens, infertility and its treatment will be easier to understand. In the next several chapters, we will look at causes of and treatments for infertility.

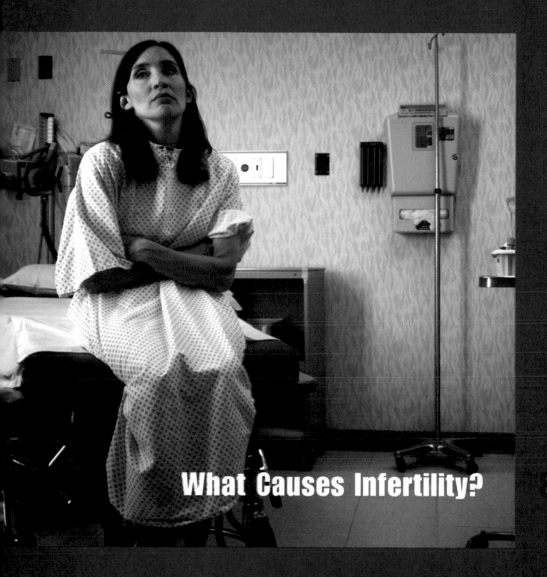

What Causes Infertility?

Life would be much easier for infertile couples if there were just one answer to the question of what causes infertility. If all infertility were caused by a single condition and could be cured with a single treatment, all infertile couples with access to the treatments would be happy parents!

Unfortunately, the world of infertility is not that simple. Even in couples who have no fertility problems, only about fifteen of one hundred women will become pregnant in any given month of unprotected intercourse.[1] If there are problems, that number drops and can reach zero.

There are many different reasons for infertility. Some affect women. Some affect men. Some affect both partners. Some can be treated easily. Some require more advanced treatment. Some cannot be treated at all. Finding the cause, and therefore the best treatment, can be like a detective investigation.

In this chapter, we will look at some of the most common causes of infertility, including information on preventing some of them.

Male Infertility Factors

"Forty percent of infertility is from a male factor," says Dr. Brian Bear, an obstetrician/gynecologist who works with infertile couples. "That can mean low sperm count, bad swimmers (we call that decreased motility), or abnormally shaped sperm."[2] To understand those factors, we need to look at male anatomy, both external and internal, and how sperm are made.

The exterior male organs. The exterior male sexual organs include the **penis** and the **testicles**. The testicles, also called the testes, are two glands inside a pouch of skin called the **scrotum**. Both testes are busy every day producing millions of sperm inside tiny coiled tubes called **tubules**. Sperm move from the tubules into a structure called the **epididymis**, behind the testicles, to mature. When a man is aroused sexually, the sperm from the epididymis move into a tube called the **vas deferens**, which takes them from the testes (hanging outside) into the inside of the body.

The interior male organs. The sperm flow from the vas deferens into two sacs called the **seminal vesicles**. There the sperm are mixed with fluid to form semen. The semen travels down the urethra in the man's penis (the same tube that carries urine out of the body) until it is expelled from the penis in an act called ejaculation. If they are not ejaculated, the sperm are reabsorbed into the body.[3]

If they are ejaculated into a female partner, the sperm begin the long journey toward the waiting egg. The woman's egg can live for twelve to twenty-four hours after ovulation. The sperm can live inside a woman's body for up to six or seven days.[4]

There are several different problems with sperm that can make a man infertile, including not having enough sperm, having sperm that are abnormally shaped, or having sperm that cannot swim well so they cannot reach the egg. In addition to sperm problems, a man can be infertile due to structural problems in his reproductive system. A bulging vein, called a varicocele, in his scrotum can make the temperature in his scrotum too hot for normal sperm production. Scars caused by sexually transmitted diseases (STDs) can block one or more of the internal tubes. Diseases such as mumps or injury can damage the testes.[5]

The statistics for male infertility can be broken down into the various causes: 40 percent is due to varicose veins in the scrotum, 10 percent to infections, 5 percent to anti-sperm anti-bodies, 2 to 3 percent to blockages in tubes, and 2 percent to hormone problems. Another 30 percent is due to unknown factors.[6]

> There are many different reasons for infertility. Finding the cause, and therefore the best treatment, can be like a detective investigation.

One recent study showed that being either too fat or too thin could also affect a man's fertility. The study, done in Denmark on sixteen hundred men, showed that sperm counts were 28 percent lower than average in very underweight men and 21 percent lower in very overweight men.[7]

Some doctors think that problems with sperm are increasing due to levels of environmental pesticides that mimic hormones. Others think inadequate nutrition can be a factor.[8] These views are controversial, and not all doctors agree with them.

If there were a single cause of infertility, there would be many more happy parents like these.

Female Infertility Factors

Women's reproductive systems are complex. In order to understand the many problems that can cause infertility in a woman, it is necessary to understand female reproductive anatomy. As with males, part of the female system is outside the body and part is inside.

The external female organs. The female external genital area is called the **vulva.** It consists of the mound of tissue that covers the pubic bone called the **mons pubis.** Under it are two sets of liplike structures called the **labia** that cover two openings into the body. One is the urethra, which carries urine out of the body. Below it is the opening to the **vagina.**

The internal female organs. The **vagina** is the canal that leads into the body. During sexual intercourse, the penis enters the vagina and the man ejaculates the sperm there. The vagina is also the canal the baby travels down during childbirth. The vagina leads to the **cervix,** the mouth of the **uterus.** The cervix is doughnut-shaped, with an opening for menstrual fluid and sperm to pass through; it can also stretch to allow a baby to pass during childbirth. The uterus is shaped like an upside-down pear. It is made of muscle and is lined with soft tissue rich in blood vessels to nourish a growing baby. The **fallopian tubes** extend from each side of the uterus near the top; they are open at the opposite end. These open ends lie close to the ovaries with their many eggs, one of which is released every month. The egg is swept into the open end of a fallopian tube. As it travels down the tube toward the uterus, it may meet the male's sperm and conception may occur.[9]

Because there are so many parts to the female reproductive system, there can be many reasons for infertility. The general categories into which problems fall are:

- structural (involving the fallopian tubes or uterus)

- hormonal (the various hormones not working correctly)

- ovarian (the ovaries not having eggs or not releasing them)

- other or unknown.

Structural. The most common factor in female infertility is fallopian tubes that are blocked with scar tissue so that the egg cannot travel down them, according to Brian Bear. "Tubes can be damaged in several different ways," he says. "Some ways are not preventable. A woman can have a ruptured appendix or an abscess that creates scarring in the abdomen."

Another cause, he says, is a disease called endometriosis that affects about 10 percent of women. In this disease, the tissue that lines the uterus moves outside the uterus and attaches itself to other organs. It can attach to the ovaries, to the outside of the uterus, or to the intestines and bladder. The misplaced tissue gets thicker and sheds each month just as it would inside the uterus, often causing intense pain. Endometriosis can cause scarring at the ends of the fallopian tubes or on the ovaries.[10]

Another major cause of blocked tubes, according to Bear, is infection with a sexually transmitted disease. "The two most common infections that cause tubal blockage are chlamydia and gonorrhea," he says. "The biggest problem is with chlamydia. Doctors call it the 'silent infertility specialist.' We call it silent because often women who have it do not have symptoms."[11]

Left untreated, sexually transmitted diseases can lead to a major infection in the abdominal cavity called pelvic inflammatory disease (PID). PID causes inflammation of the fallopian tubes, uterus, and the ovaries. It is most common in women younger than age twenty-five who have many sexual partners. Even if a woman has just one partner, if that partner has many other partners, she is at risk. PID is the most common preventable cause of infertility. The risk of becoming infertile doubles each time a woman has it. It is treated with antibiotics. The woman's partner must be treated also to prevent reinfection.[12]

Preventing Infertility From Tubal Scarring

The best way to prevent tubal scarring is to prevent infection with sexually transmitted diseases. The only 100 percent effective method is not having sexual intercourse. A sexual relationship with only one partner, who also has no other sexual partners, is safe if both partners are disease free. Some types of contraceptives offer some protection from STDs. Barrier methods such as condoms, diaphragms, cervical caps, and sponges can reduce the risk, especially if they are used with a jelly that kills sperm. However, they are not foolproof.[13]

Brian Bear points out that it is important to treat an STD with antibiotics early before it causes scarring. It is also important for a person who is treated to come back four weeks later for a follow-up test to be sure he or she is cured. It is also important for a woman who is treated for an STD to tell all her sexual partners so they can be treated. She should not have sexual relations again until they are.[14]

Hormonal. If the complex interplay of hormones is not working correctly, pregnancy may not occur. A woman must be producing enough of four key hormones to become pregnant: follicle-stimulating hormone (FSH), which matures the egg; estrogen, which gets the uterus ready to accept the fertilized egg; and progesterone and luteinizing hormone (LH), which help it to implant in the uterus wall. Low levels of any of these hormones may mean that the woman is not releasing any eggs or that a fertilized egg may not be able to be implanted.

Ovarian. A woman cannot become pregnant unless there is a healthy egg to fertilize. There can be several reasons why a woman may not ovulate or ovulate irregularly. It is possible, though rare, for a woman to be born without eggs in her ovaries. The hormones that are required to mature an egg may be out of balance. A woman who exercises excessively or does not get adequate nutrition can cause her weight to drop. If her percentage of body fat falls below 22 percent, she may not ovulate and periods may stop. Severe stress can also play a role. Some women's ovaries form cysts; she may not ovulate normally. Some of these conditions can be treated with drugs. If a woman's weight loss is due to an eating disorder called anorexia, she may need professional help.

Other reasons. Perhaps the most common factor in the "other" category is the woman's age. A woman's fertility actually peaks at age eighteen. However, peak fertility continues through most of her twenties and then starts a slow but steady decline. At age thirty-five, fertility has declined significantly. A third of women at this age will have problems getting pregnant. Over age forty, two thirds will deal with infertility.

Dr. Brian Bear meets with a patient. Dr. Bear treats infertile couples as well as patients without fertility problems, and he counsels teens about sexual health.

As women age, their eggs age as well. Women who become pregnant later in life have a higher risk of miscarriage. While younger women have a 15 to 20 percent chance of miscarriage, those in their early forties have a 34 percent chance, and women over age 45, a 53 percent chance of miscarriage. Being able to become pregnant, but not able to carry a baby to term, is not true infertility, but can have the same affect on a couple who want a child.

Men can father babies later in life, beyond the time when women can become pregnant. But their fertility also declines as they age.

In today's world, women often wait to start a family until they are established in careers. That can be a worthy goal. But women who make that decision need to know the statistics. Eighty percent of women under age thirty-five will be pregnant in a year of trying. Of the 20 percent who are not, half will have easily treated infertility issues and will be pregnant within two years. The other half will need "higher tech" help to become pregnant. For women over age thirty-five, it is harder, may take longer, and may require much more high-tech help. In their late thirties, only 10 percent will become pregnant in any given month, over age forty it is 5 percent, and at age forty-five only one percent. Yet 20 percent of all first-time mothers are over age thirty-five, so it is not impossible.[15]

There are also some lifestyle factors that may contribute to infertility:

- Caffeine seems to affect fertility in both men and women. Too much caffeine can make it harder for the woman to become pregnant and may produce abnormal sperm in the man.

- Smoking is generally bad for health but can also affect fertility. Women smokers have more trouble conceiving and have a higher risk of miscarriage. Certain chemicals in the smoke can damage sperm.

- Drinking alcohol can damage a woman's eggs. If done during pregnancy, it increases the risk of miscarriage and can damage the fetus.

- Using marijuana and cocaine can damage sperm.

- Using hot tubs can lower a man's fertility by raising the temperature in the scrotum and damaging the sperm. Wearing tight underwear every day may do the same thing.[16]

Then there is the final, and most frustrating, cause of infertility: unknown. In 10 to 15 percent of cases the doctors will simply say, "We do not know why you are not becoming pregnant." More than one woman has struggled with unknown infertility, sometimes for years, and then, suddenly, become pregnant. Doctors cannot say why that happens either. Some things in the human body remain a mystery.

How Is Infertility Diagnosed?   4

Diagnosing what is wrong inside the human body would be a lot easier if doctors had a window to peek into. Unfortunately, that is not how the human body works. Finding the cause of infertility can be a challenge. Most of the female reproductive system is hidden away inside where it cannot be easily seen. Even the male system has enough inside structures to make finding a problem difficult.

Doctors who work with infertile couples can be from a number of different specialties. For the woman, the doctor can be a gynecologist (specialist in health care for women) who has a subspecialty in reproductive endocrinology (hormones). For the man, the doctor will usually be a urologist (specialist in disorders of the urinary and reproductive systems) or an andrologist (specialist in male infertility).[1]

Couples who are trying to conceive without results should not wait too long to seek help, according to Estril Strawn, M.D., director of reproductive endocrinology at the Medical College of Wisconsin. "If the woman is under thirty-five years of age, she should wait for one year," he says. "If she is over age thirty-five, she should only wait for six months. There is a real decrease in a woman's ability to get pregnant as she gets older, so we want to help women who are having difficulty early on."[2]

When a couple comes to Strawn for help in finding the reason they are not conceiving, the first step, he says, is always a thorough health history and physical exam. "We need basic information about the things that allow a woman to become pregnant and a man to father a child," he says. "We need to know that the woman is producing eggs and having regular menstrual periods and that the man is producing semen that has sperm in it."[3]

Some of that information can be gathered just by asking questions. A woman will be asked about her menstrual history. She will also be asked about previous pregnancies, previous abortions, sexually transmitted diseases, pelvic infections, or any kind of abdominal surgery. The man will be asked when he first became able to ejaculate, if he has ever fathered a child, and if he has any history of sexually transmitted diseases or mumps. He may also be asked about the use of drugs, including illegal drugs and steroids, since certain drugs can lower fertility. Some of the questions for both men and women may be very personal and uncomfortable to answer, but the doctor needs full information for a diagnosis. Couples should also remember that any information they give a doctor remains strictly confidential.

After the health history, the doctor will do a basic physical exam to see if the reproductive structures that can be seen or felt appear normal. For the woman, this will probably include an internal, or pelvic, exam in which the doctor inserts an instrument called a speculum into her vagina. That allows him or her to see partway inside the reproductive tract and to better feel the position of the uterus and ovaries.

If all seems to be normal, the next step is further testing to get information about the reproductive structures and the couple's hormonal systems. Generally, the man is the first to be tested because the tests done on him are less invasive (they do not require going inside the body) than the tests for women. If the problem is his sperm, the woman may not have to have as many invasive tests.[4]

The Male Fertility Workup

The main test for fertility in a male involves taking a close look, under a microscope, at his sperm. The man provides a sample of his sperm by ejaculating into a sterile container. If he does this at home, the specimen must be taken to the office or clinic immediately. The doctor evaluating the specimen under the microscope will be looking for several things:

- Sperm count. Normal males produce huge numbers of sperm in every ejaculation. Anything between 20 million and 100 million sperm is considered fertile. Anything under 20 million is considered a low sperm count. Males with low sperm counts need to understand that having a low count does not make them less masculine. Men with low counts, or even no sperm at all, can have normal sexual function. Low sperm counts can be caused by birth defects (part of the production equipment is missing), abnormal hormone levels, illness (including STDs), or use of marijuana or anabolic steroids.[5]

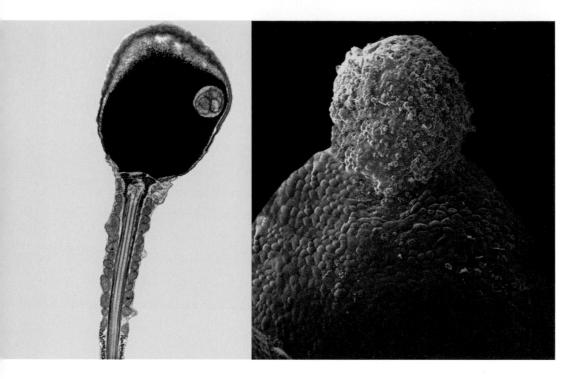

These microscopic images show the head and midpiece of a human sperm (left) and the ovulation process (right).

- Motility. This term refers to how well the sperm are able to swim toward the woman's egg. Infection, illness, or use of drugs such as marijuana and even tobacco can cause sperm to swim poorly. To be considered normal, at least 60 percent of sperm need to swim normally.[6]

- Morphology. This term refers to the shape of the sperm. A sperm has three parts: the head, which contains the DNA; the midpiece, which contains the energy for the sperm to swim; and the tail, which makes the sperm move. Abnormality in any of these areas can result in infertility. A sperm with abnormal DNA will not be able to fertilize an egg, and a sperm without enough energy to "go the distance" or one with a coiled tail instead of a whiplike tail will not be able to reach the egg in time.[7]

- Clumping. Sperm that stick together in tight little clumps are not normal. Clumping can be a sign that the man's body is making antibodies against his own sperm. Antibodies are cells that attack outside invaders such as bacteria or viruses. But in some cases, the body can, for unknown reasons, begin to see part of itself as an outside invader and attack. In this case, the man's body can be attacking his own sperm.

- High white or red blood cell counts. High counts of various types of blood cells in the semen can indicate infection somewhere in the reproductive system.[8]

It is possible for sperm to be normal in one category but abnormal in another. For example, a man could have plenty of sperm, but slow swimmers. Or he could have normal swimmers with poor shape.

Sometimes, a man's problems with sperm are such that it is hard, but not impossible, for him to father a baby. That man would be called subfertile rather than infertile.

Another common problem, responsible for up to 40 percent of male infertility, is a bulging vein, called a varicocele, in the testicle. A varicocele can be corrected with microsurgery—a surgical procedure done with a microscope and very small instruments.[9]

One other area the doctor will look at is the man's hormone levels. While not as complex as the female reproductive hormone system, the male still needs to have the right levels of four different hormones to be fertile. Some of the hormones, surprisingly, are the same as female hormones. They are FSH, LH, prolactin, and testosterone. Low levels can be treated with drugs.[10]

At the end of the male workup, the couple may or may not have an answer to their fertility problem. If the male has no sperm at all, he will not be able to father a child. In that case, the couple has several choices. They can use sperm donated by another man, they can turn to adoption, or they can decide not to have children. If he has only a few sperm, or the sperm cannot get out of his testes, the sperm can be removed with a needle and used for in vitro fertilization. If the man has some other problem that can be corrected, they can have that done and then resume trying to conceive. If the male is normal with no problems, the couple has the option of moving on to testing the woman.

The Female Fertility Workup

A female's reproductive system is more complex than a male's, both in structure and in hormone balance. Therefore, testing is more difficult, time consuming, and expensive than that for a man. There are many tests, ranging from least to most invasive. Generally, unless the doctor suspects a particular problem, he or she will begin with the least invasive test and move on to more invasive ones. Doctors know that about 30 percent of female infertility is due to hormones, and 50 to 60 percent is due to structural problems. That may also influence the order in which the tests are done.

Here is a list of the most common tests used in diagnosing female infertility. Different doctors may use them in a different order:

- Blood tests for hormone levels. Doctors can test a blood sample for a variety of different hormones.

- Testing for ovulation and normal mucus. Sometimes a woman who is not making eggs also does not menstruate, but it is possible to have normal periods without egg production. So one of the first things a doctor will want to know is whether or not a woman is ovulating. She can easily test for this at home using a home ovulation test kit. Then she will have an ultrasound in the doctor's office to see if her ovary is making a large follicle from which an egg can erupt. A blood test for progesterone level is done seven

Dr. Estril Strawn, director of reproductive endocrinology at the Medical College of Wisconsin, counsels patients. Dr. Strawn says couples should not wait too long to seek medical help if they are having problems conceiving.

days later to make sure a mature egg was released. In addition, all women have a certain amount of mucus in their cervix, the entrance to the uterus. The doctor will test to see if that mucus is the right consistency to allow the sperm to live while it passes into the uterus. The doctor takes a sample of the woman's mucus and looks at it under a microscope. The pattern it forms when dry tells the doctor whether or not it is normal. If it is not, estrogen may correct the problem.

- Testing for levels of other hormones. The doctor may look at the hormones that are released at each stage of the woman's monthly cycle. Some hormones that are out of balance can be corrected with medication. Some cannot.

- Testing for infection. Infections in the reproductive tract, or in other parts of the body, can affect fertility.

If none of these tests pinpoints the problem, it may be a structural defect or blockage. The best way to diagnose structural problems is to "take a look" using several different tests to actually look at a woman's reproductive organs.

Ultrasound. Ultrasound uses sound waves. The waves are "bounced" off organs, and the pattern they create makes a picture of the organ. The test is often used during pregnancy to look at the fetus. An ultrasound test can tell the doctor about the size and shape of the pelvis and pelvic organs and can show anything unusual.[11]

HSG. This test has the tongue-twisting name of hysterosalpingogram. It is an X-ray test that outlines the uterus and fallopian tubes so that the doctor can tell if their shape is normal and if the tubes are open. The test is done by injecting dye into the uterus through the cervix. The dye spills out of the uterus into the tubes while the doctor watches on an X-ray machine. If the dye does not come out, it means a tube is blocked. Sometimes, if the woman has a minor blockage in her tube, the test itself will clear it.

Hysteroscopy. If the doctor wants a really close look at the inside of the uterus, he or she may use a special scope called a hysteroscope. It is guided through the cervix and into the uterus itself. The doctor can see any small growths or scar tissue and even remove them.

Laparoscopy. While a hysteroscopy looks inside the uterus, laparoscopy gives the doctor a look at the whole abdominal cavity. Under general anesthesia, a lighted scope is put into the abdomen through one or more tiny incisions. Looking around the abdominal cavity, the doctor can see abnormalities in the uterus or tubes, scar tissue, and endometriosis. If a small amount of endometriosis is found during a laparoscopy, the doctor can remove it. Severe endometriosis may require treatment with drugs and then more surgery.[12]

> **At the end of the male fertility workup, the couple may have the answer to their fertility problem. If not, they have the option of testing the woman.**

Some doctors use a postcoital test at the time of ovulation. First, the couple has intercourse, then reports to the lab or doctor's office. The doctor collects the sperm from the mucus around the cervix to see if they are surviving and swimming normally. That test, however, is not used as much as it used to be because the results are not always reliable.

Another specialized test is to see if the woman's body is producing antibodies against her partner's sperm. If she is, the couple may use a condom for several months to allow her body to clear the antibodies before trying again. The sperm can then be put directly into her uterus to bypass the mucus and antibodies.[13]

After both workups, most couples will know what is causing the problem. They will then need to make some decisions about what kind of treatment they are willing to have. Some may be simple, such as taking a medication. Some may be complex, invasive, and expensive. Not all couples may be willing to go down that path.

About 15 percent of couples will not get an answer even after complete workups. Their diagnosis will be "unexplained infertility." That diagnosis can be very difficult for the couple. While it is good to know that nothing is wrong, it is very frustrating when pregnancy still does not happen. About 20 percent of couples with unexplained infertility will conceive in the next year.[14] The rest may never have an answer. They will need to look at options such as ART, adoption, or living without children.

Most couples going through this experience can benefit from counseling to help them handle the stress. Finding out that you are infertile can cause serious issues of guilt, anger, and lowered self-image. If it is a male problem, the man may think, "I'm not a real man if I cannot give my wife a child." If the problem lies with the woman, she may think, "What kind of a woman am I if I cannot have a child? I am a failure." Those kinds of thoughts are very destructive to a relationship and can cause a marriage to break up.

Many fertility specialists include a counseling component in their workups and treatment. "Infertility is a crisis," says Gloria Halverson, M.D., a gynecologist who specializes in infertility. "It's on a similar level to divorce, illness, or death in the family. The emotions vary with the couple, but commonly we see anger. We see guilt and shame. We see deep sadness over losses, especially the loss of the couple's dreams."[15]

There are some destructive ways couples use to deal with the emotional stress of infertility, says Barbara Reinke, Ph.D., who counsels Dr. Halverson's infertility patients.

> One is blaming themselves or their partner. Another is what psychologists call negative self-talk, thinking "I'm a failure, I'm worthless, my spouse would be better off with someone else." Some people dull the pain with alcohol, or desperately spend too much

Members of three generations of one family pose for a photograph. The ability to pass on one's genes to the next generation is important to many people; when something goes wrong with the process, they may blame themselves.

money chasing the next procedure even when the odds of success are low.[16]

Instead, Reinke says, couples should stop and look at what it is that makes them valuable people. "It's not just being a parent that make[s] a person valuable." She points out that when a couple is in a crisis over infertility they may feel very alone. They need to realize that others have dealt with the same problem. They should take advantage of sources of help such as support groups. "Talking to others can help couples realize they are not alone, that what they feel is normal, and that their future is still bright and has meaning no matter the outcome of the infertility treatment," she says.[17]

Experts who have worked with couples dealing with infertility issues warn that there are several signs that the emotional aspect is taking too great a toll. They include:

- Mood swings
- Withdrawal from friends, especially friends with children
- Never doing anything for fun
- Seeing their lives as revolving around infertility, rarely thinking or talking about anything else
- Not being able to have intercourse that does not involve the "right" day
- Worrying constantly about paying for the treatments
- Becoming depressed: not wanting to do things that have been enjoyable in the past, experiencing changes in appetite and sleep patterns, feelings of guilt, anxiety, or overwhelming fatigue, changes in concentration or memory, even thoughts of suicide.[18]

One woman summed up her emotional struggle by saying:

Infertility is a series of steps of giving up your dreams; first you give up the dream to conceive naturally. Then some give up the dream of conceiving a biological child; some then give up the dream of being pregnant and feeling their child live inside of them, then giving birth; some then give up the dream of giving love to a child. Each step brings a different set of decisions, a whole new world of emotions. And we all pray not to progress to the next step in the chain.[19]

It is very important for couples having such stress reactions to see a counselor for help in dealing with them.

If the couple who has received a diagnosis decides to go ahead with treatment, they will enter a world of choices. In the next chapter we will look at those choices: how infertility is treated.

Making Babies the High-Tech Way

When a couple has completed the infertility tests, exhausted as they may be, they face a whole new set of decisions. Depending on their diagnosis, the treatments range from simple and not very invasive to complex procedures that require expensive drugs and microsurgery.

Couples first must decide how important having a baby is to them. Are they willing to give fertility drugs a try? How about having the sperm washed, concentrated, and placed into the woman's uterus? If that will not solve their problem, are they willing to go the "highest tech" route and have their baby conceived in a plastic dish, and then have the embryo placed into the woman's uterus?

All these options have risks and side effects. None is easy; all are costly. Some insurance covers the treatments, some does not. There are no guarantees of success. At the end of the process, the couple may be left with a thinner wallet and no baby. But all those disadvantages have to be weighed against the best possible outcome: a baby.

Different couples make different choices. For some, the desire for a biological child is so overwhelming that they are willing to do anything it takes, bear any cost, any discomfort, to reach their goal. Other couples may be willing to do the lower tech treatments, but they draw the line at in vitro fertilization, the "test-tube" baby. Some couples are willing to do one round of IVF, but not more. Other couples decide to skip the whole thing and try to adopt a child. Others decide that having a child is not as important as they first thought, and they can have full, happy lives without being parents. Each couple has to decide what is right for them, and no other person has the right to make a judgment about their decision.

Standard Infertility Treatments

Like infertility testing, treatment is different for males and females. Treatments also differ depending on the cause of the problem.

Treating male problems. If a man has no sperm, or abnormal sperm, he may be completely unable to father a child. Most often, such problems are not correctable. A couple with that type of problem can choose to use another man's sperm to fertilize the woman's egg, creating a child that is her biological child but not his. If the man's problem is caused by structural defects in the system of tubes that carry sperm or varicocele in his testicles, it may be possible to correct the problem with microsurgery.

If the problem is low sperm count, sperm that do not swim well, or the presence of antibodies against the sperm (which either he or his female partner can make), the sperm can be given a nudge to get them to do their job. The sperm can be placed into the woman's uterus instead of getting there through normal sexual intercourse.

As a part of several different infertility treatments, the man's sperm may be treated to give them the best possible chance to reach the waiting egg. The sperm are collected as the man ejaculates into a sterile container. The ejaculate is washed and the sperm concentrated, according to Rachel Mann, Ph.D., an

Myths About Infertility

Over the centuries, people have believed some very strange things about encouraging conception:

- Going swimming on the first day of your marriage means a woman will get pregnant.

- Leaving a diaper under the bed means a pregnancy.

- If you are the first to visit a newborn, you will be the next to be pregnant.

- Eating peanut butter during the last two weeks of your menstrual cycle will encourage a pregnancy to "stick."

- Smelling behind a pregnant woman's ear will help you conceive.

- Holding a newborn for a day will increase your chances of conceiving.

- Standing on your head for ten minutes after sex increases the chance of conception. (There may be some truth to this, since the sperm have to swim "upstream" to reach the egg, but doctors usually say that staying bed with the hips raised for a short time is enough.)

- Touch a fertility statue from an ancient culture to become pregnant.

- A hot bath before sex will relax your reproductive tract and make conception more likely.

- Hanging a man's hat on the bedpost will ensure pregnancy.[1]

embryologist who did many assisted reproduction procedures at an infertility treatment center. The term "washing sperm" may sound like they are cleaned with soap and water, but that is not the case. "Doing that would kill them," Mann says with a laugh.

> Washing means we remove all the fluid that makes up the semen. There may be white blood cells and cells other than sperm in the fluid. When we "wash" the sperm, we remove everything except swimming sperm cells. That is usually done by spinning the ejaculate in a centrifuge [a device that spins at high speed]. A small pellet is created at the bottom. The pellet is the concentrated sperm. At the top is all the junk you don't want.[2]

In a sense, the process is like the spin cycle on a washing machine, spinning off the water and leaving the clothes at the bottom. The concentrated sperm can be placed in the woman's reproductive tract or can be used to fertilize her eggs in a dish.

Treating female problems. Because female infertility can have so many causes, there are also many different treatments. If the infertility workup has shown that the woman has an abnormal reproductive system, one with missing or abnormal parts, the problem may not be correctable, and she may not be physically capable of carrying a pregnancy to term.

If the diagnostic tests show that the woman's fallopian tubes are blocked with scar tissue, and the tissue was not "blown out" by the dye in the test for blocked tubes, they may be opened with delicate microsurgery. In many cases, the blockage is due to endometriosis. It can be treated with drugs, or the deposits can be removed with surgery, often using a laser to burn them away.

If the woman is not ovulating, fertility drugs can prompt her ovaries to release a mature egg. The most commonly used fertility drug is called Clomid. It causes the ovaries to produce more than just one egg a month. That is why women taking Clomid or other fertility drugs have a higher-than-normal chance of

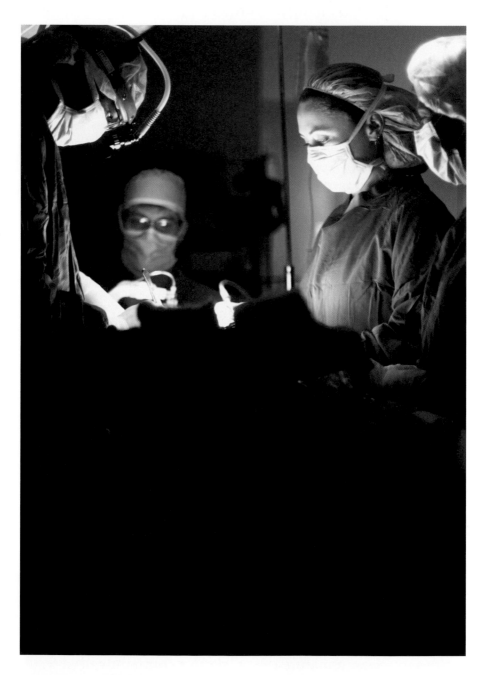

Some types of infertility in women can be treated surgically. If scar tissue is blocking the fallopian tubes, they can often be opened with microsurgery. Laser surgery can be used to treat endometriosis.

having more than one baby. About 60 percent of women who are not ovulating will produce eggs using Clomid.[3] If that type of drug does not work, the next step may be more powerful drugs called gonadotropins, which must be injected. Using those drugs is often called ovarian hyperstimulation because the ovaries are put into "overdrive," so to speak. Fertility drugs, especially the more powerful gonadotropins, can have unpleasant side effects. A woman taking them may experience premenstrual-like symptoms, including headaches, weight gain, and mood swings.[4]

Assisted Reproductive Technology (ART)

Once it is established that the woman has eggs and her partner has live sperm, or that the couple are willing to use eggs or sperm from a donor, the couple may enter the world of assisted reproductive technology (ART). ART refers to any procedure that brings egg and sperm together in some way other than by normal sexual intercourse. Some doctors are now using the term "assisted conception," but no matter what it is called, it means helping the egg and sperm to get together to create a baby. ART procedures range from placing the sperm into the woman's body to creating an embryo in a dish.

Intrauterine Insemination (IUI)

IUI is a type of artificial insemination—the placement of sperm in the woman's reproductive tract through a method other than sexual intercourse. (Other ways include placing the sperm in the vagina or in the cervix instead of directly into the uterus.) It is the low-tech end of ART procedures. The actual procedure is quite simple, according to Mann. The woman lies on a table with her feet in holders called stirrups, which elevate her knees. Mann explains:

The sperm, washed and concentrated, are introduced through her vagina, through her cervix using a catheter, a long straw-like tube that is used to suck up the sperm and inject them. Only washed sperm can be put directly into the uterus. In normal sexual intercourse, the ejaculation takes place in the vagina and the sperm swim through the cervix where they are "cleaned up." Normal ejaculate cannot be put directly into the uterus because of risk of infection and cramping because of things other than sperm in the fluid. When you wash the sperm you are getting the best quality sperm and you are able to put them as close as you can to the egg.[5]

Even if the woman is taking fertility drugs, an IUI procedure has a success rate of 10 to 20 percent on each cycle, Mann says. "It depends a lot on the woman's age," she adds. "If she is over age forty, it is almost pointless to do an insemination. Even after thirty-five there is a lower rate of success."[6] The best chance is for a woman under age thirty. Each couple is different, however, and each cycle can be different.

It is interesting to note that while sperm washing is a relatively new treatment, doctors have been doing artificial insemination for almost a hundred years. The first known use of insemination was in 1909; it caused a huge controversy at the time.[7] It is also widely used in the world of animal reproduction; semen from prize bulls or horses is used to create many offspring.

In Vitro Fertilization (IVF)

In July 1978, the world was astounded to read about the first test-tube baby, Louise Brown, who was born in England. She was called a test-tube baby because of the mistaken impression that the egg and sperm were united in a test tube. Actually, a petri dish, a flat plastic dish used in laboratories, is used. Brown's birth marked the beginning of the ART revolution. It has grown ever since. The number of IVF babies born in the United States has quadrupled from 10,924 in 1994 to 45,000 in 2002, the most recent year for which statistics are available from the Centers for Disease Control and Prevention.[8]

IVF is the highest level of ART. Couples who opt for it know they will spend a lot of money if their insurance does not cover it. The woman will endure some discomfort, and they will have no guarantee of coming out with a baby. Yet thousands of couples every year are willing to take the risk for the possibility of becoming parents.

IVF is much more complex than IUI, even though the man's sperm are collected and washed in the same way. Getting a woman's eggs is much more complicated than getting sperm, since the woman does not have a way to eject them from her body. Instead, the doctor must go inside to get them. Therefore, IVF is a four-step procedure:

Step 1. The woman gets ready by taking fertility drugs for the first two weeks of her cycle, usually the injected gonadotropins. The drugs cause a large number of eggs to mature instead of just one. During these two weeks, she sees the doctor about every two or three days for ultrasounds and a blood test to check her hormone levels.

Step 2. The woman's eggs are retrieved. The eggs must be collected (which is called *retrieval*) at the point where they are mature and ready to be released. According to Mann, eggs are usually retrieved through a procedure called transvaginal aspiration. She explains:

> The woman lies down on the table. The doctor has an ultrasound machine with a screen that creates an image of her abdomen. They can see how many follicles are in her ovaries. The aspiration equipment is a suction tube connected to a long needle. An ultrasound probe is hooked up to the needle as well. The whole unit is inserted into the woman's vagina. Once the doctor locates the ovaries, the needle is punctured through the side wall of the vagina at an upward angle. The doctor inserts the needle into the follicle and sucks the eggs out. It's like using a vacuum cleaner. An assistant holds the other end of the tube, collecting the eggs and

the fluid around them in test tubes. The tubes are passed to the lab where they are immediately emptied into culture dishes and the contents inspected to see if there is an egg.[9]

Eggs are usually taken from both ovaries. Mann says that the woman can be asleep under general anesthetic, awake with a local anesthetic, or have no medication, although general anesthesia is most common. Some women find the procedure painful, other women do not. "The puncturing of the vagina can be like getting a shot," she says. "In addition, some women's ovaries are more sensitive to pain than others."[10]

The doctor will retrieve as many eggs as possible to avoid having to go back for more. A poor egg retrieval will yield fewer than five eggs; an excellent cycle will yield as many as twenty-five to thirty, Mann says. An average cycle will yield ten to fifteen.[11]

Step 3. Fertilization is a critical step; if the eggs and sperm do not join, there will be no embryo. Mann says:

> Once you have the eggs, you put each one into a round plastic dish the size of a bracelet filled with a culture media[a solution especially blended to keep egg and sperm alive] and put them into the incubator to recover. The media tries to duplicate the environment the egg or embryo would be in while inside the woman. The exact recipe depends on what you are putting into it. If the media is for sperm, it's one recipe. If it's for eggs, it's another recipe. If it's for early embryos, it's still another.[12]

The egg retrieval day is called Day Zero, she says. Usually the fertilization is done in the afternoon of Day Zero. About seventy-five thousand washed sperm are put into each dish with an egg. Day One is the next morning, when the egg/sperm mixture is evaluated to see if the eggs have been fertilized. Mann explains:

> That day they would be at the one-cell embryo stage. It's still just one cell, but it's not an egg anymore. It's an embryo. When the male and female DNA unite they form two little circles called pronuclei you can see under a microscope. Early on Day One you can see two pronuclei—that's a good fertilization.[13]

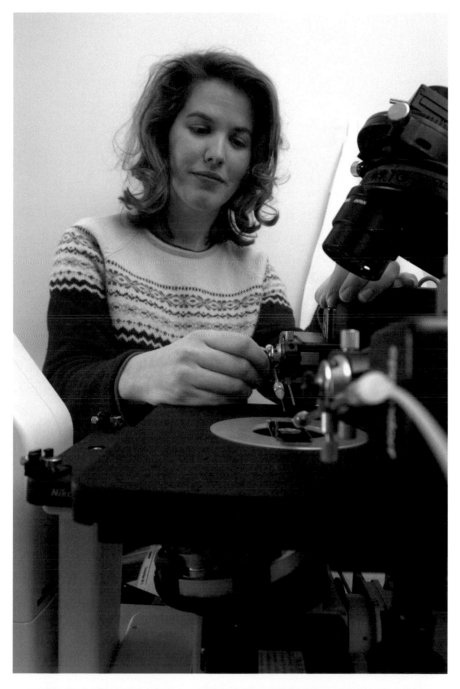

Dr. Rachel Mann is shown using an injection microscope. Dr. Mann worked in the field of ART, helping infertile couples to achieve their dream of having a baby.

The embryos grow each day. On Day Two the embryos should be two to four cells. Each day the number of cells doubles until they reach a stage where you cannot really count the cells anymore. The cells start to compact, or merge. Fluid starts to enter the embryo. This is called the blastocyst stage. "It's amazing to see," Mann says. "The blastocyst looks kind of like a soccer ball with a hollow center filled with fluid and the cells on the outside."[14]

Different facilities use different procedures, but generally the embryos are cultured for three to five days. More centers are moving to Day Five transfers when the embryos are at the blastocyst stage because the media to grow them has improved in the last few years, and it is possible to grow them in the dishes a little longer, Mann says.[15] During these days, the woman takes the hormone progesterone to thicken the uterine wall and get it ready for the embryos to be implanted.

Step 4. Transferring one or more embryos from their individual dishes into the woman's uterus may begin a pregnancy. If the embryo becomes implanted, the uterus will be its home for the next nine months. Of course, not all the embryos will be transferred. There is a debate right now in reproductive medicine about how many embryos to transfer. Transferring more than one gives a greater chance of pregnancy. But multiple-fetus pregnancies create many problems, and some or all of the fetuses may not survive. Some couples are willing to take a chance on transferring multiple embryos and are willing to abort some if too many become implanted. Other couples are not willing to do that. Since multiple pregnancies create many ethical and moral issues, it is important that the couple and their doctor discuss all the possible outcomes and the issues they raise before the transfer is done.

Since not all the embryos created are going to be transferred, the embryologist will choose the most healthy-looking ones. That is done by examining them carefully under a microscope.

"At the blastocyst stage we can pick out the better quality embryos," Mann says. "Poor quality embryos usually will not develop to that stage. We can transfer fewer embryos because we know the ones we are using are good quality."[16] The remaining embryos will usually be frozen for future use. The ability to freeze extra embryos has created ethical and moral issues (especially regarding disposal of unused embryos) that our society is just beginning to debate.

The transfer process does not take much time. On transfer day, the woman will again be in the same position on the table. The ultrasound machine will again allow the doctors to see the position of her uterus. Often the woman's husband is present to

Risks in IVF

Nothing in life is risk-free. Neither is high-tech conception. Here are some of the risks faced by couples who use IVF:

- A higher-than-average risk of pregnancy with more than one fetus. Twin births happen naturally about one percent of the time. In IVF pregnancies the rate is 25 percent. Pregnancies with multiple fetuses have an increased risk of miscarriage and premature delivery.

- Increased risk of ectopic pregnancy, in which the embryo implants in a fallopian tube. As the fetus grows, the tube ruptures, which can be a life-threatening emergency. IVF pregnancies have twice the risk of ectopic pregnancy.

- Birth defects. The risk of increased birth defects in IVF babies is controversial. Some studies show increased risk, others do not. More research is needed.[17]

- Emotional problems. Infertility causes much emotional stress and can put strain on a relationship. IVF failure or deciding to end treatment can cause grief. People may blame themselves, their partners, or they may worry that their partner may leave for someone who is fertile. Many couples need counseling to cope with the stress.[18]

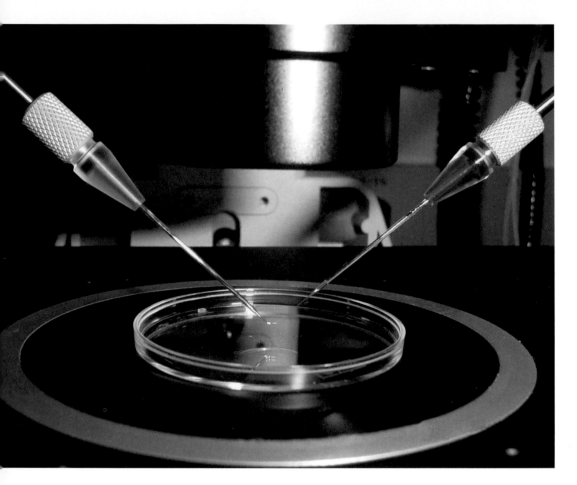

This equipment allows an embryologist to hold an egg in place, then pierce the outside of the egg and deposit a single sperm.

see the transfer, since most clinics are aware how important this moment is to the couple. Mann says:

> The embryologist looks through a microscope and loads the embryos into a catheter. It's done as quickly as possible because the embryos have to be at a certain temperature so they can't be out of the incubator too long. The embryologist then walks the catheter over to the physician. He or she inserts it through the woman's cervix into the uterus, then presses a little syringe to inject the contents of the catheter into the uterus. The goal is to place the embryos near

the tip of the uterus without actually touching the walls because that might disturb the lining. It's an amazing process to watch.[19]

The woman rests on the table for a half hour or so, then she is free to go home. She usually is advised to take it easy for a couple of days. The wait begins. Usually it takes two weeks to see if the IVF has "taken"—if any of the embryos have been implanted. The woman has a blood test two weeks later to see if she's pregnant; then, if she is, she's tested to see if she needs hormone supplements to support the pregnancy.

While a standard IVF seems complicated enough, there are two additional procedures that can be done to help increase the odds of pregnancy.

Intracytoplasmic sperm injection (ICSI). If a man has very few sperm or they are too weak to penetrate the firm "shell" that forms the outside of the egg, there is a technique to help the sperm penetrate the egg. The method was developed after a doctor in Belgium who was working with IVF accidentally pierced a human egg and discovered that piercing did not kill the egg.[20] ICSI is done under a very high-power microscope. The embryologist chooses one sperm, the best one, from those available, breaks the tail and sucks it into a very fine needle using a micromanipulator. "The embryologist moves it with his or her hands like the joystick you use to play a video game," Mann explains. "He or she penetrates through the egg's shell into the inside of the egg. Then he or she injects the sperm inside the egg and hopes for the best!"[21] This technique offers hope to men who were thought to have no sperm in their ejaculate. Some of those men actually have a few sperm in their epididymis and testes. Doctors can sometimes surgically extract sperm for injection into the egg.[22] This procedure is also used with a low sperm count or if there are only a few eggs. It raises the chance of fertilization, avoiding wasting eggs if there are only a few.

Assisted hatching. When the blastocyst implants into the uterus, it first must break out of its "hard" shell, called the zona. The zona protects the embryo as it travels through the fallopian tubes down to the uterus and prevents more than one sperm from entering the egg. Sometimes in older women, or with embryos that have been frozen, the shell is harder than normal. That embryo may need a little help to break the shell so it can implant in the lining of the uterus. Doctors have found a way to give an embryo with a stubborn shell help in breaking through. "The embryologist can make a tiny hole in the shell," Mann says. "Sometimes it is done with a laser, sometimes it is done with a drop of acid. You want more than a puncture, you want a small opening. It is done microscopically using micro-manipulators."[23]

Preimplantation genetic diagnosis. One more factor can come into play in an IVF procedure. With today's technology, doctors can look at the embryos before transferring them and screen out those with certain genetic defects. Mann explains:

> If an embryo is harboring a fatal gene, or something that could cause a miscarriage or some kind of chronic illness, we can find that out. We can do a genetic analysis on one of the embryo's cells. We are already doing it for a certain number of known genetic diseases such as hemophilia or Tay-Sachs disease and some others. If a couple knows they are at risk, we can use this procedure on the embryos before they are transferred and make sure we transfer only ones without the genetic defect. Right now we can test for only a handful of things, but in the future we will be able to do that better.[24]

This ability to do genetic testing before transferring an embryo raises serious ethical and moral issues. Some people feel it is unethical to choose certain embryos over others because they are more "perfect." Other people think it is unethical to choose an embryo because it is of the sex the parents want. Other people see no problem in making those decisions. These questions will only be resolved after serious debate and discussion.

Other factors that affect success. Researchers have found several outside factors that may affect success with IVF. In a study of women done in Boston, very overweight women had a one-in-five chance of an IVF embryo implanting, while in normal-weight women, the chance was one in four.[25] The woman's age is also a big factor: The older the woman, the lower her chances of success.

When a Couple Cannot Become Parents Themselves: "Third-Party" Reproduction

Sometimes, after all the testing is done, the couple gets really bad news. For some physical reason, they cannot have a biological

There are many ways to have a family. The woman on the right adopted a daughter from Korea (the woman on the left), who then went on to have her own child.

child and carry the pregnancy themselves. Perhaps the man has absolutely no sperm. Or the woman's ovaries are not capable of making any eggs. Perhaps she is making eggs, but due to her age, they are of poor quality. Perhaps she has no uterus, or an abnormal one that cannot sustain a pregnancy. Or perhaps she can become pregnant but has repeated miscarriages. Is there any hope for these couples outside of adoption or deciding not to be parents?

The answer is yes, if they are willing to use a third person to supply the missing factors. "Third-party reproduction" means using someone besides the couple—a third person—to help them achieve their goal of being parents. Some people do not consider third-party reproduction to be a form of infertility treatment. One psychologist who counsels infertile couples says, "Donor programs are legitimate and wonderful ways to build families, but they are not infertility treatments per se.[26] However, for the purposes of this book, we will consider third-party reproduction part of the array of choices available to couples with infertility.

If IVF raises ethical and moral issues, it is nothing compared to the questions raised by third-party reproduction. Some people see the introduction of a third party as immoral—they feel it is the equivalent of infidelity. Others have no such qualms. Legal issues can become very complex: Who is the "real" father or mother, or the legal parent, in a situation in which a third person's egg or sperm have been used? If the third person is the one to carry the fetus, is she entitled to change her mind and keep the baby? These issues are very difficult and divisive and are presently being debated in society and in the courts.

The costs, risks, and side effects of infertility treatments have to be weighed against the best possible outcome: a baby.

When the man has no sperm. If a man produces no sperm at all, he is called sterile. Birth defects, diseases such as mumps, or treatments such as chemotherapy for cancer can all leave a man sterile. If he and his partner want to experience pregnancy, they will need to use sperm supplied by another man. It will be placed in the woman through artificial insemination. This is called donor insemination. Donor insemination became possible in the 1950s, when the technology to collect and preserve donor sperm was developed. When doctors found they could freeze sperm and it would still be alive when thawed, the possibility of "banking" sperm became a reality. The first commercial sperm bank, in which donors were paid for their sperm (and recipients also paid for it) opened in the early 1970s.[27] Donors arc scrccncd for health issues before their sperm is accepted. Recipients can request sperm from a donor who resembles themselves physically. A baby born from a donor insemination will be the biological child of the mother, but not of the father.

When the woman has no eggs. When a woman either has no eggs or has eggs of poor quality due to her age or some other factor, it is also possible for her to experience a pregnancy. However, the process is more complicated than that using donor sperm; it requires an IVF procedure. "Eggs can be obtained from another woman who is proven to have normal egg production," says Dr. Estril Strawn of the Medical College of Wisconsin. "That woman agrees to have her eggs removed from her body. They are put into a dish and fertilized with sperm from the man and the resulting embryo is put into the body of the woman who has no eggs."[28] The resulting baby will be the father's biological child, but not the mother's. Donors are also screened for genetic issues and can be matched to the recipient's characteristics.

In most cases of either donor eggs or donor sperm, the donor and recipient do not know each other, Strawn points out. "But in some cases the donation is directed, which means the woman or the man chooses another woman or man who has

This boy was born from an embryo (shown at left) that was donated by a couple who had more than they needed.

agreed to be the donor," he says.[29] In some cases, relatives or friends have donated sperm or eggs. Sperm donors are paid by the sperm bank, and the couple pays the bank, he says, while egg donors are often paid directly by the couple receiving the donation. While there are ethical issues surrounding payment, it is generally accepted that donors can be compensated for their time and, in the case of an egg donor, discomfort and risk. Payment amounts vary widely, but payment for a sperm donation is in the hundreds of dollars, while payment for an egg donation may be in the thousands.[30]

If neither partner is able to contribute egg or sperm, the couple may use an IVF embryo created from donor eggs and donor sperm. In that case, the resulting child will not be the biological child of either parent. Sometimes couples who have undergone IVF successfully but have "leftover" frozen embryos will donate them to a couple who cannot supply either egg or sperm. Some infertility clinics have active "embryo adoption" programs in which prospective parents are screened. That means they are interviewed and visited in their homes to make sure they would be good parents, just as they would be if they applied to adopt a child. In the case of a donor embryo, the resulting child would be the biological child of the donor couple, not of the parents. As you can see, the combinations of biological and donor children can become quite complicated. It also raises some thorny ethical and legal issues, which are being debated within our society and legal system.

Using a gestational surrogate. If a couple have both viable eggs and sperm but the woman cannot carry a pregnancy because of physical problems, the couple may turn to hiring someone to carry the baby for them. Some people have laughingly referred to this form of third-party reproduction as "rent-a-womb." But for the couple involved, it is not a laughing matter. Couples who want to find a surrogate mother have a lot of questions to answer before making the decision. Should they use someone they know? Sisters, cousins, friends, and even mothers have carried their relative's child to give the couple the gift of parenthood. Or should they hire a surrogate they do not know? What legal issues are they likely to deal with? Laws vary from state to state, but generally the law says that a couple may only pay reasonable medical costs for a surrogate. If the surrogate changes her mind after the child is born, to whom does the child belong? Couples usually have some type of contract with the surrogate. But if she changes her mind, the contract may not hold up in court.[31] Different courts in different states have given different rulings. But one thing is the same in all such cases: a great deal of emotional pain for all the parties involved.

Some couples want to be very involved with their gestational surrogate during the pregnancy. They are present at doctor appointments and watch closely to be sure she is eating a healthy diet and doing everything else she can to have a healthy baby. Many times the couple is present at the baby's birth. When the baby is placed into their arms, the couple can feel that it is truly "theirs."

Couples in the past had no choices about reproduction. Either a woman became pregnant and the couple had a family, or they did not. There were no options except adoption. Today, as we have seen, couples face a wide array of choices. They can be complex and difficult. But those choices also offer great hope to couples who want to have children. Today, there certainly is more than one way to do it!

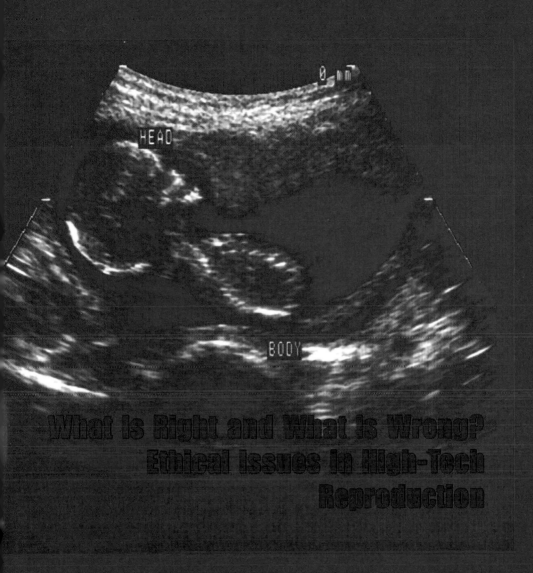

HEAD

0 mm

BODY

What Is Right and What Is Wrong? Ethical Issues in High-Tech Reproduction   6

High-tech reproductive technologies give people a chance to be parents. How could anyone object to that? But in actuality, some things that are done in the world of ART are very controversial. Intelligent, thoughtful people who wish only the best for people trying to become parents can sincerely differ on some of the ethical issues ART raises. There are times when the lines between "right" and "wrong" can seem very shadowy.

For example, the Roman Catholic Church does not approve of any conception that happens outside the human body. Thus, intrauterine insemination is acceptable, but in vitro fertilization is not. Orthodox Judaism does not allow either. Other religious groups have different standards, and some take no position on these questions at all.

We will look at the different ethical questions. Our goal is not necessarily to determine what is "right," but to raise the questions and point out where the law stands at this writing (laws are changing rapidly and may be different by the time this book is read). Our guides in this process will be Gloria Halverson, M.D., a fertility specialist who has strong reservations about some aspects of ART; Robyn Shapiro, a lawyer in private practice who is also a medical ethicist at the Medical College of Wisconsin; and the positions taken by the American Society for Reproductive Medicine, the association that most fertility specialists belong to. "Technology is morally neutral," Halverson points out. "It's what you do with it that can cause issues."[1]

Availability of Treatment

Who should get infertility treatment? Anyone? Only those who will be "good" parents? Should couples have to be married? What about single women who want a baby? What if a single man wants a child using a surrogate mother? What about same-sex couples? Should health insurance have to pay? That means everyone insured will pay higher premiums so someone can be a parent. Is that fair? If insurance does not pay, does that mean only the wealthy will be able to have children using ART? Is that fair? If a doctor knows that the chance of pregnancy is tiny, say one or 2 percent, is it right for him or her to take a couple's money even if they want to try?

Take the issue of "good" parents. Should doctors decide whether or not a couple will be fit parents before agreeing to help them become pregnant? Robin Shapiro says:

> Some states require a nonmedical evaluation, much like a home study before adoption, but not all. The law does not say that

couples have to be married, but some clinics do require that. Some insurance companies say they will cover infertility treatment only for married couples, or only for cases in which they are using the wife's eggs and husband's sperm. That can raise issues of discrimination.[2]

Halverson recalls reading about a case in which a man in prison struck up a relationship with an old high school class-mate and they wanted to have a baby. Since she was too old to use her own eggs and since the prison did not allow conjugal visits (allowing inmates private time to have a sexual relation-ship), they approached an IVF center. They were turned down.[3]

The American Society for Reproductive Medicine has con-sidered the issue of doctors choosing which patients to accept and which to reject. In a paper on reproductive medical ethics published in the journal *Fertility and Sterility*, they said, "Physicians [may] decline to accept individuals as patients as long as they do not violate laws against impermissible discrimi-nation."[4] Obviously, that means a doctor cannot say no based on the person's race or religion.

But what about when the issue is whether or not to provide expensive treatment when the chances of success are very low? The Society says that doctors may ethically refuse treatment to such patients. It recommends that fertility centers should develop policies and standards about accepting or refusing patients in advance. Once those policies are in place, prospective patients should be aware of them and all decisions should be based on those guidelines.[5]

How Many Embryos to Implant

As we have seen in previous chapters, when a couple is attempting IVF, there are often many eggs harvested, many embryos created, and more than one transferred at a time. That creates an ethical issue. Halverson says:

The more embryos you transfer, the higher the success rate. But then there is the worry of multiple births. That's a big debate in reproductive medicine right now. It is being legislated in some countries: In England and Sweden you are only allowed by law to transfer one embryo. In our country we have guidelines, but it is not a law.[6]

The issue is not an easy one. Statistics say that the rate of multiple births increased 400 percent after the development of IVF. However, guidelines by the American Society for Reproductive Medicine suggesting no more than two embryos have cut the rate of multiple births. Births of triplets or more fell by a third between 1997 and 2000, according to a study reported in the *New England Journal of Medicine*. Some doctors worried that reducing the number of embryos transferred would hurt chances of conception, but because of advances in technology, the rate of live births for IVF actually increased during those years, the study said.[7]

Still, the guidelines do not have the force of law. Fertility doctors can transfer more embryos. What if many embryos are transferred and so many "take" that the mother is at risk of losing all of them, or they will be so small at birth that they may not survive or have severe handicaps? In such cases, some doctors will perform an abortion called selective reduction to remove one or more of the fetuses. Some parents are willing to do that; some are not. Some doctors and clinics are willing to do that, some are not. The individual decisions are usually based on when the couple or the doctor believes that life begins. "Most guidelines agree that embryos are human life," Halverson says. "The issue is whether you think it is OK to sacrifice one [fetus] for the benefit of the other."[8]

According to Shapiro, there is no legal definition of when life begins:

It is not so much an issue of when life starts but an issue of when the rights of personhood [begin]. If a state passed a law that rights

These identical twins were not born through ART. The incidence of multiple births increased following the introduction of high-tech fertility treatments.

of personhood begin at conception it would probably be challenged in court under *Roe* vs. *Wade* [the Supreme Court ruling that declared abortion, with certain restrictions, legal in the United States]. But there is no hard and fast law outside of interpretations of *Roe* vs. *Wade*. Different people have different opinions on when rights [begin].[9]

Shapiro points out that the question is best answered before the issue of selective reduction arises. "Should there be greater regulation of how many embryos are transferred?" she asks. "Limiting it has been done in other countries for some time now. I myself think there is a lot of sense in limiting how many you transfer."[10]

What to Do With Unneeded Embryos

Having too many embryos in the uterus is not the only ethical issue that IVF creates. Another question is what to do with the "leftovers." If a woman has many eggs harvested, many can be fertilized. The embryos that are not transferred are put into frozen storage. A recent survey of fertility centers surprised a lot of people when the number of embryos in frozen storage was totaled: nearly four hundred thousand! About 88 percent of them are being kept for the couples who created them to use for future pregnancies. About 2 percent have been earmarked for donation to other couples, another 3 percent for medical research. The rest are in a sort of limbo—the couples who created them do not know what to do with them or have abandoned them.[11]

The question of who legally owns the frozen embryos is a thorny one, especially if the couple divorces or one person dies. "That has been the topic of many court cases," says Shapiro. She notes:

> Some courts say that a written agreement about that must be followed, and many, but not all, clinics require such agreements. But other courts have said such agreements are not binding because the circumstances have changed. In some cases courts have ruled that someone cannot be forced to become a parent against his or her will, despite any previous agreement. So you can't say who legally owns them because it varies from state to state and from court to court.[12]

What to do with the embryos can be a wrenching decision. There are basically only three choices, Halverson says: "Donation, destruction, and using for research."[13]

Sue and John DiSilvestro are an example of a couple facing this dilemma. They have triplets and do not think they want any more children. But they have three embryos in frozen storage. They are agonizing over what to do with them. Sue would possibly be willing to donate them for research, but John is not.

"Everything changes once you have kids," he told a reporter. "I now realize those embryos are my children. It's a different ball game."[14] Couples with embryos in storage can spend hundreds of dollars a year on fees while they try to decide.

Option one, destroying the embryos, is a problem for many couples because they believe the embryos are human life and their children. Other couples have no such beliefs and are willing to have their excess embryos discarded. A survey of 217 fertility clinics asked how they dispose of excess embryos. Seven clinics said they performed a semireligious ceremony including a prayer for each one. Four insisted that the couples be present when the embryos were destroyed; several others would not allow the couples to be present. Thirty-three clinics did not destroy embryos at all; almost all the clinics were willing to store the frozen embryos permanently. Four clinics said they gave the frozen embryos to the couples to either destroy themselves or store in their freezers at home. Seven clinics said they never create more embryos than they intend to transfer, so they have no extras.[15]

Donating the spare embryos is a good option for many couples. Three quarters of the clinics in the survey allowed couples to donate spare embryos to other couples.[16] One adoption agency that places donated embryos, Snowflakes, had twenty-seven babies born and an additional eighteen on the way in June of 2003 when they spoke to a reporter.[17] However, some couples are not willing to have a genetic child raised by another couple that they have no contact with.

Donating the embryos for research is also an option for some couples and not for others. Sixty percent of clinics in the survey allow that option.[18] Researchers know that human embryonic stem cells (the cells in the inner lining of an embryo) have not yet become the type of cell (hair, skin, etc.) that they will eventually become. They think that the cells, if put into a person who has some cells or organs that are not working, could become the type of cells, or even organs, the person needs. They want to find out if those cells could be useful in treating a variety of diseases, including diabetes and Parkinson's disease. No one knows if it will work; only a great deal of research will tell the story. Taking the cells for research kills the embryo. Some people think it is acceptable to sacrifice embryos for the research they hope will save lives. Others, like Halverson, say destroying a human life, no matter how early, to save another life is morally wrong. "I think scientifically life begins at fertilization because at that point you have a genetically unique human being," she says. "I don't think it is morally or ethically correct to use them for research, but some people do."[19]

The American Society for Reproductive Medicine has tackled this difficult problem. They find such research acceptable providing certain guidelines are met. Their recommendations, which do not have the weight of law, are that couples must know about the research project their embryos will be used in, they need to understand that their embryo will be destroyed in the process, that whenever possible someone other than their treating doctor should ask for the embryos (to avoid a conflict of interest), and that embryos should never be bought or sold.[20]

Genetic Selection of Embryos to Transfer

It is now possible for doctors to extract a single cell from an embryo before transferring it and find out certain things about the baby it would become. Today doctors can learn the child-to-be's sex and whether or not it will have certain defects that are caused by genes. In the future, doctors may be able to learn much more. That presents another ethical dilemma. Is it morally acceptable to choose embryos with certain genetic characteristics and to discard others? The debate has centered mostly on sex selection because some genetic defects are carried only by one sex, and it is not always possible to test for the individual defect. Most people seem to agree that when a genetic defect is

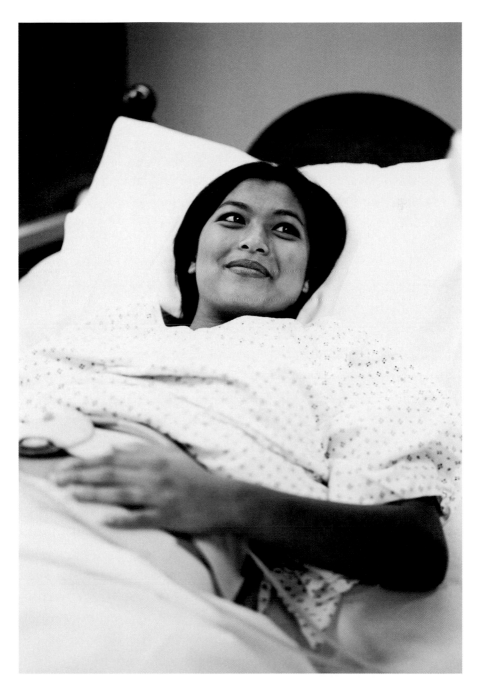

A pregnant woman is being monitored to make sure her baby is healthy. Because of different opinions over when life begins, many aspects of ART are controversial.

present and it can be tested for, it is acceptable to select embryos that do not carry it.

Shapiro says:

> Genetic selection is worrisome because it could be the first step down the road to eugenics—making the fetus look or be as we want it to look or be. On the other hand, if you have a known disease that is linked to one sex and you want to know if an embryo is male or female to avoid bringing into life a child with a terrible disease, then I think finding out is very appropriate. I do have a problem with "I have three boys and I want a girl." Because then we are not talking about actions to eliminate suffering and disease, but rather enhancements. That's scary—it's a slippery slope.[21]

Halverson actually has to deal with those kinds of requests from patients. She says:

> Again there is no one right answer. It is the new eugenics, not mandated by government to wipe out a certain people as in the past, but by parents who understandably don't want a child with a genetic disease. Obviously you would not choose that embryo. But wanting a boy or a girl, or a certain hair color—those I won't do.[22]

The American Society for Reproductive Medicine has taken a stand on preimplantation sex selection. They say sex selection to prevent the transmission of serious genetic defect is ethically acceptable. But sex selection for nonmedical reasons "gives cause for serious ethical cautions." Therefore, they say, it should be discouraged, but not legally prohibited.[23]

As if the issues swirling around what to do with embryos are not enough, when you enter the world of third-party reproduction, more issues arise. Who should be donors, and how much should they be paid? Whose child is it—the donors of the genetic material or the parents who are raising it? Should a woman who gives birth to a child have any rights if she has just "rented out her uterus" and has no biological connection to the child? Besides ethical issues, these kinds of situations raise legal issues as well, and they can become *very* complex as different

This tank holds frozen embryos that are being donated to infertile couples. States deal in different ways with the issues raised by the donation of sperm, eggs, and embryos.

combinations of donors and infertile couples are formed. We will separate these issues into donor issues and issues of surrogacy.

Donor Issues

If a man donates sperm anonymously and it is used to create a baby with the wife of a sterile man, who is the father? This issue was once fairly easy to resolve, says Shapiro. "Most states have dealt with that by saying that if a woman is artificially inseminated with another man's sperm and is legally married at the time, her husband is presumed to be the father of the child," she says.[24] But, she points out, courts are seeing more children who want to know who the anonymous donor was. More clinics are now keeping records of where sperm are used, and some states, she says, are thinking about requiring records to be kept and access provided to the children. One sperm bank in California offers identifying information to children when they reach age eighteen; others offer to contact the father without giving his name to the children, again when they are eighteen, to ask him if he wants to share information about himself or meet his biological child. In at least one state, Washington, a court has ruled that a sperm donor has no legal rights or responsibilities unless there is a contract in place saying that he does.[25]

One other issue can arise—if a sperm bank provides many donations in the same area, children who are actually half brothers and half sisters could meet later in life and marry. Most sperm banks try to have clients over a wide geographical area to avoid that situation.

With egg donors, a different issue arises. It's simple for a man to provide sperm, and for that reason payment has usually been minimal, in the hundreds of dollars. But for a woman to donate eggs requires heavy-duty ovary-stimulating drugs and an invasive procedure to retrieve them. So payment for egg donors has been higher, in the thousands of dollars. But how much is too much? At what point are you no longer compensating a woman for her risk and trouble but buying human eggs? "In order to assure that her decision was not coerced, there is need to see that the payment is not undue," Shapiro says. "Some states have laws to prevent payment above a reasonable level. But knowing what is a reasonable level can be a problem."[26]

The American Society for Reproductive Medicine has weighed in on this issue. They recommend that payments to women donating eggs should be "fair and not so substantial that they become undue inducements that will lead donors to discount risks." They also say the donor should have her own doctor, not the recipient's doctor, to avoid conflicts of interests. They advise fertility clinics to refuse to participate if donors have been paid an excessive amount.[27] All of this, however, does not stop Web sites that offer eggs, with photos of beautiful women, for very high prices.

Some couples are lucky enough to find an egg donor who does not want any money at all. Allison, a Florida woman, is an egg donor for her cousin and husband. "I am not being paid," she writes. "I don't intend to ask for money. My cousin and her husband have been trying to have a baby for over 10 years. If this works, that will be payment enough."[28]

Her wonderful gift, however, raises still another issue. Should family members be donors? That can be confusing in a family. Allison will be the genetic mother of her cousin's child. Will she want some say in how the child is raised? Will the child some day be told, "Cousin Allison is really your mother?" The same can be true for sperm donations within a family. A man can be the genetic father of his relative's child. Things can become very complex. "I think anyone who wants to do a donation within a family would need careful psychological screening and counseling to be sure they have considered all the issues," says Halverson.[29]

This baby was born from a donated embryo. Couples with "extra" embryos decide whether to store them in frozen form, donate them to other couples, or donate them for medical research.

On the issue of telling the child his true biological parentage, Mary Casey Jacob, Ph.D., director of the University of Connecticut's infertility program, encourages her clients to tell the child the truth. "Keeping secrets is hard and most of us are lousy at it," she points out. "Most couples do not anticipate how many lies must be told in order to do so."[30]

Halverson agrees. "But if you are going to tell the child, you should do it when the child is old enough to understand," she says. "There may be an issue if you tell a lot of other people— at a family party someone may say to the child, 'He's not your father, Uncle John is your father.' That's not a good way for the child to find out."[31]

The American Society for Reproductive Medicine says that donations within families should be allowed except in relationships where, if the pregnancy occurred naturally, it would be considered incest. Therefore, a brother should not be allowed to donate sperm to inseminate his sister if her husband is sterile, because a brother/sister relationship would be incest. The same holds true for fathers donating sperm to daughters, or mothers donating eggs to a son's wife.[32]

Issues With Surrogacy

When an infertile couple asks another woman to carry their child for them, a whole group of additional issues is raised. There are two types of surrogacy: gestational surrogacy and true surrogacy.

If a woman has usable eggs but cannot carry a pregnancy because of a defective or missing uterus, the couple may have an embryo created through IVF and have it transferred to another

One Complex Case

An Arizona couple, after trying for many years to have a child, finally hired a surrogate mother they found on a Web site. The young woman who took the job did it to earn extra money for her family. The agreed-on fee was $15,000. The embryos were created with the infertile couple's eggs and sperm. The IVF center transferred five embryos to the surrogate's uterus telling the two couples that there was a one-in-three chance that one would "take." Fast-forward a few months. The surrogate had an ultrasound—it showed five growing fetuses! Both families were shocked.

Nationwide, a little over five hundred babies were born through the use of surrogates in 2002, according to the Centers for Disease Control and Prevention. Not many such pregnancies result in such a high number of babies.[33]

The surrogate mother in this case has decided not to accept payment from the infertile couple. She feels they will have enough of a financial burden with five babies. "It will be reward enough," she said, "to see them go home with five healthy babies.[34]

woman's uterus. This is called gestational surrogacy. Sometimes such an arrangement is jokingly called "rent-a-womb"; the resulting baby is the genetic child of the parents and has no genetic relationship to the surrogate.

If, however, a woman has no eggs as well as being unable to carry a pregnancy, the surrogate can be inseminated with the husband's sperm. The resulting baby is the genetic child of the surrogate and has no genetic relationship to the infertile woman. This is called true surrogacy; it raises the most ethical and legal issues.

Both of these forms of surrogacy have created legal issues in the past. According to Shapiro:

> We've seen a couple of high-profile cases about surrogate payment. There are laws against being paid for putting your child up for adoption, that's called black market baby buying. Some states say you can reimburse a surrogate for expenses only. But some women say, "I'm providing a service here and I'm a big girl, I can make up my own mind about this." Clearly, inordinate payment raises red flags. But it isn't explicit in law yet. There are, however, states that prohibit paying brokers [people who bring together future parents and surrogate mothers]. I think that's probably a good idea.[35]

Halverson points out that parents who are using a surrogate may want to have control over what the surrogate does. Will she be allowed to smoke? Drink? What if she takes drugs? "There is a risk of the surrogate bonding with the baby—what if she wants to keep it?" she says. "Some states define the 'mother' as the person who gives birth to the baby; in those states the genetic mother must adopt the baby."[36] Halverson sees even greater issues with a surrogate who is the genetic mother of the baby:

> That procedure can become nonmedical because you don't need a doctor to inseminate the surrogate with the husband's sperm. Anyone can do it, or the husband and surrogate could have normal intercourse. Then, if the mother changes her mind, the baby is genetically hers. The baby can become a consumer item. I remember a case in which the baby had birth defects; the couple

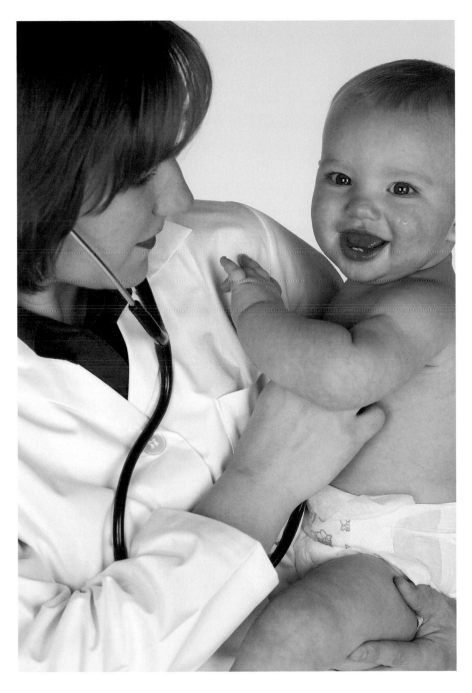

A healthy baby is the goal of every pregnancy. In surrogacy or donor arrangements, the issues become more complicated.

would not take it and the surrogate didn't want it. I have the greatest issues with this type of surrogacy.[37]

When a surrogate changes her mind and wants to keep the baby, a lengthy court battle can take place. "Some states have laws that make contracts between the parents and the surrogate unenforceable," says Shapiro. "Others don't; they say the contracting couple are the parents. It can be a real legal mess." She recalls a case in which the court actually ruled that the baby had no legal parents! In that case, a donated embryo was used with a surrogate, so no one had a genetic connection to the child. Before the baby was born the intended parents divorced, and the wife sued the husband for child support. The intended father said the surrogate was the real mother so he did not owe his ex-wife any money. A higher court ultimately reversed the lower court ruling and said the intended parents were the legal parents.[38]

As these cases illustrate, surrogate relationships can be legally very difficult and can cause immense pain to the families involved. That is not to say that using a surrogate is wrong. In many cases, it works well. But all parties need to know the risks and enter into the relationship with their eyes open.

The American Society for Reproductive Medicine has no problem with surrogates unless they are family members in which the relationship, if it happened naturally, would be considered incest. Thus, a sister should not be a surrogate for her brother's child or a daughter a surrogate for her father's child.[39]

"These issues are so difficult because our capabilities are evolving so fast that it's hard to keep up with medicine, much less anticipate the ethical and legal questions and address them in time," Robyn Shapiro sums up. "Technology gets ahead of ethics; that's it in a nutshell."[40]

Brave New World: Coming Advances in Infertility Treatment

When Louise Brown, the first test-tube baby, was born in 1978, no one could have foreseen the incredible advances in infertility treatment available today. No one guessed that less than thirty years later doctors would inject sperm into eggs and drill holes in embryos to help them "hatch."

What will the future bring in the field of reproductive technology? No one knows. And given the speed of change in the last thirty years, we can only guess what changes babies born today will see in their lifetimes.

But a few people are willing to make that guess.

Preimplantation Genetic Diagnosis

Rachel Mann, the embryologist who did many IVF transfers, says that in her opinion, preimplantation genetic diagnosis (finding out if an embryo carries a genetic defect before transferring it) is the most significant recent advance. She thinks the next advances will be in that field. "We are already doing it for a certain number of known genetic defects. But now there are only a handful of diseases we can test for. In the future we'll be able to do that better and more efficiently. I think that's a really good thing."[1] However, that is also a very controversial thing.

As we have seen, some people feel it is unethical to select embryos with certain characteristics and discard others. While many people do not have a problem with doing so to avoid genetic diseases, many do not find it ethical to select for sex or physical characteristics such as hair or eye color. If and when we find a gene for things such as musical, artistic, or athletic ability (or even for more controversial things, like sexual orientation) the debate on preimplantation diagnosis is sure to become even more heated.

Artificial Womb

Asked if we will ever have an artificial uterus that can carry a pregnancy to term, Mann says, "We are nowhere near that. Maybe some day, but not in our generation."[2] If that ever becomes possible, it will raise a whole new set of issues. Should women be able to have their fetus develop in an artificial womb to avoid the inconvenience of pregnancy and childbirth? If embryos are created to use their stem cells, will it be ethical to keep the embryo to the fetal stage and "harvest" its cells or organs? At what stage—three months, six months, nine months? The issues will be difficult and emotional.

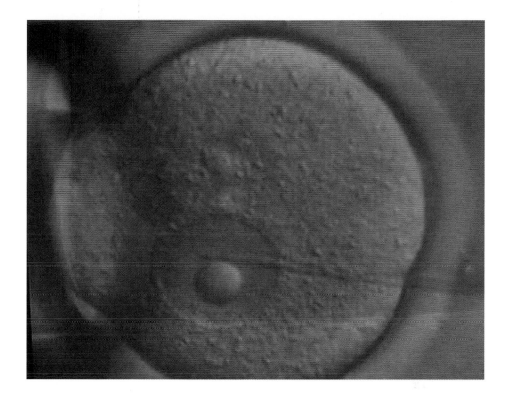

This photo shows a mouse ovum being injected with sperm. Research on other animals has contributed to the ability of scientists to achieve ART for infertile couples; similar research will be conducted to solve the problems that remain.

Freezing Eggs

It would be helpful to women if they could freeze their eggs for later use. A woman might want to do so if she was going to have a medical treatment of some kind that might damage her eggs. Or a woman might freeze her eggs when she is young so she has the option to use them later in life. Sperm and embryos have both been frozen successfully for many years. But freezing eggs has been more problematic, because they contain so much water. Water turns to ice crystals, and that can damage the eggs.

In the past, doctors have been able to freeze part of an ovary with eggs inside for women who are about to undergo chemotherapy. Recently, methods of freezing eggs alone have been developed. In procedures that are now being explored, women take drugs to stimulate their ovaries. Their eggs are harvested and then frozen, to be thawed when the woman is ready to become pregnant.

Scientists note that the technique is still in its infancy and is not very successful yet. The American Society for Reproductive Medicine has recommended that egg freezing be limited to clinical trials.[3] But there are a number of clinics that offer this service to women, and a number of babies have been born following the procedure. At least one pregnancy has resulted from an egg donated by another woman.[4]

Cytoplasmic Transfer

One technique that has been tried but not perfected involves injecting the cytoplasm (contents of an egg cell) from a younger woman's egg into the egg of an older woman. The cytoplasm does not contain the egg nucleus, so the baby that would develop would be the older woman's genetic child, but the egg would be younger and better able to be fertilized. Some children have been born with this technique, but there was a high rate of a particular birth defect among them. Such transfers are now being researched to be sure children born of them will not have defects.[5]

Cloning

In cloning, a genetically identical copy of the original organism is produced. Twins are an example of clones that occur naturally. The technique of cloning is too complex to cover in this book, but some of the ethical questions that occur with assisted reproduction apply to cloning as well.

At the current time, cloning human beings is not permitted in many countries, including the United States. In some countries such research is permitted, and a cloned human being may

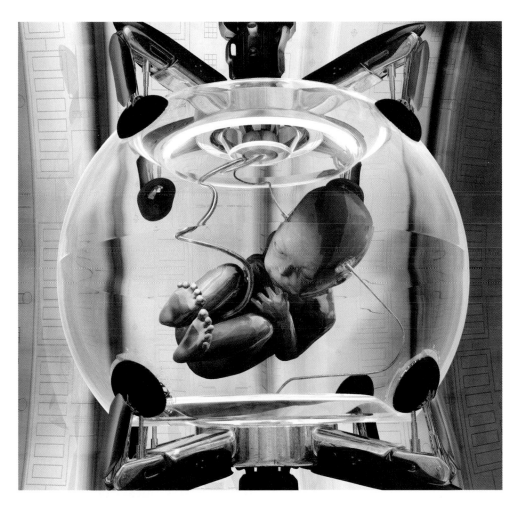

One artist's view of what an artificial womb would look like. Scientists say that such inventions are far in the future, if they ever exist.

be born in the near future. Cloning in animals has resulted in high rates of birth defects and disease later in the animal's life. Dolly, a sheep, was the world's first cloned mammal; she was the only successful clone born in three hundred tries. She started to get arthritis when she was only six years old and had to be destroyed because she was aging much faster than normal. Other animal cloning has produced a few successful births and many failures.

What the future will bring in this area is very hard to know. Whatever it is, it is certain to bring more debates: Is it ethical to create a human being in such a way? Will a clone be considered a full human being? Will it have legal rights? Is it permissible for parents of a child who dies to create a clone of that child? Would that be an emotionally healthy thing to do—for the parents and for the new child? What about a man or woman cloning a dead spouse, or a child cloning a dead parent—even though the clone would be a baby, not the same age as the person who died? Those will be very difficult and divisive issues for society to deal with.

Blastocyst Transfer

A blastocyst is the ball of cells created as a fertilized egg grows. Waiting until day five to transfer an embryo as a blastocyst seems to be better than transferring earlier. Only 30 to 50 percent of embryos grow to that stage, so the ones that do are probably better quality. About 70 percent of five-day embryos become implanted, while only about 50 percent of three-day embryos do. However, it is harder to grow an embryo to that stage, and not all clinics can do it. In the future, doctors will probably learn to grow the blastocyst for an even longer time. Today, blastocyst transfers have a higher rate of twin births; in the future, as researchers learn more, that may no longer be a problem.[6]

Regulating the New Technologies

As many of the ethical issues in high-tech reproduction become more common, the law will probably catch up to the technology. Future infertility clinics will probably be more heavily regulated by law, not just guidelines, than clinics are today. That may prevent some distressing legal issues from arising.[7]

The world of assisted reproduction is one that is in the process of being explored. Looking at the changes in technology and what that has done to the ability of doctors to help couples dealing with infertility, it is hard to imagine what things reproductive medicine will be able to accomplish in twenty-five or fifty years or longer. Because ethics and law typically lag behind science, it is not hard to imagine the debates that will take place in the future as even more technological achievements become available. It may be a wonderful world for couples who want to have children but cannot in the normal way. It may be a painful world for some people who see technology as violating their basic beliefs. But whatever happens, it will be an interesting world to watch.

Chapter Notes

Chapter 1   Three Couples Cope With Infertility

1. E-mail interview with "Joanna," August 6, 2004.
2. Telephone interview with "Terry" and "Jim," July 22, 2004.
3. Ibid.
4. Telephone interview with "Lynn," August 7, 2004.

Chapter 2   How Conception Happens

1. "Facts About Birth Control: Reversible Prescription Methods—
   The IUD (Intrauterine Device)—ParaGard and Mirena," Planned
   Parenthood Federation of America, April 2005, <www.ppfa.org/
   pp2/portal/files/portal/medicalinfo/birthcontrol/pub-birth-control-09.
   xml> (August 23, 2005).
2. Alicia Weissman, "Gynecology: Contraceptives," *University of Iowa
   Family Practice Handbook*, n.d., <www.vh.org/adult/provider/
   familymedicine/FPHandbook/Chapter13/01-13.html> (September 3,
   2004); and Helena Oliviero, "New Contraceptives Give Couples
   More Choices," Cox News Service, n.d., <www.azcentral.com/
   families/articles/0503fam_birthcontrol.html> (September 3, 2003).
3. "Teenage Myths About Contraception," *BBC News Health*, July 16,
   2001, <http://news.bbc.co.uk/1/hi/health/1441898.stm>
   (September 3, 2004).
4. "Menstrual Cycles: What Really Happens in those 28 Days?,"
   Feminist Women's Health Center, n.d., <www.fwhc.org/health/
   moon.htm> (September 2, 2004); and Niels Lauersen and Steven
   Whitney, *It's Your Body: A Woman's Guide to Gynecology* (New York:
   Putnam Publishers, 1993), pp. 76–80.

Chapter 3   What Causes Infertility?

1. Telephone interview with Brian Bear, July 12, 2004.
2. Ibid.

3. American Medical Association, *Complete Medical Encyclopedia* (New York: Random House, 2003), pp. 1065–1066.

4. M. Sara Rosenthal, *The Fertility Sourcebook* (Chicago, New York, San Francisco: Contemporary Books, 2002), p. 98; "Ask Planned Parenthood," August 22, 2005, <http://www.ppfa.org/pp2/portal/files/portal/webzine/askexperts/app-050822-sperm.xml> (November 10, 2005).

5. "What Should I Know About Male Infertility?" *American Family Physician*, vol. 67, no. 10, May 15, 2003, p. 2173, and American Medical Association, p. 722.

6. Rosenthal, pp. 104–105.

7. Marilyn Marchione, "Being too fat, too thin may hurt male fertility," *The Milwaukee Journal Sentinel*, October 22, 2004, p. 4A.

8. Richard Firshcin, "Spcrm Wails," *Psychology Today*, vol. 30, no. 5, September/October 1997, p. 26.

9. American Medical Association, pp. 1064–1065.

10. Ibid., p. 511.

11. Bear.

12. American Medical Association, pp. 722 and 964.

13. Ibid., p. 964.

14. Bear.

15. Jackie Meyers-Thompson and Sharon Perkins, *Fertility for Dummies* (New York: Wiley Publishing Inc., 2003), pp. 8–10.

16. American Medical Association, p. 723.

Chapter 4   How Is Infertility Diagnosed?

1. M. Sara Rosenthal, *The Fertility Sourcebook* (New York: Contemporary Books, 2002), p. 29.

2. Telephone interview with Estril Strawn, July 3, 2004.

3. Ibid.

4. Rosenthal, p. 95.

5. Jackie Meyers-Thompson and Sharon Perkins, *Fertility for Dummies* (New York: Wiley Publishing, 2003), p. 131.

6. Rosenthal, p. 102.

7. Meyers-Thompson, p. 133.

8. Rosenthal, p. 103.

9. Ibid., pp. 105–106.

10. Ibid., pp. 107–108.

11. Rosenthal, p. 122.

12. Meyers-Thompson, pp. 123–126.

13. Rosenthal, pp. 132–134.

14. Ibid., p. 140.

15. Telephone interview with Gloria Halverson, March 11, 2005.

16. Telephone interview with Barbara Reinke, August 7, 2004.

17. Ibid.

18. Rosenthal, p. 228, and American Medical Association, *Complete Medical Encyclopedia* (New York: Random House, 2003), p. 110.

19. Michele St. Martin, "Donor Egg & Sperm: A Family-Building Alternative for the Infertile," *Preconception.com: for those who are trying to conceive,* n.d., <www.preconception.com/resources/ articles/donorprograms.htm> (May 26, 2004).

Chapter 5   Making Babies the High-Tech Way

1. Jackie Meyers-Thompson and Sharon Perkins, *Fertility for Dummies* (New York: Wiley Publishing, 2003), pp. 44–45.

2. Telephone interview with Rachel Mann, July 20, 2004.

3. M. Sara Rosenthal, *The Fertility Sourcebook* (New York: Contemporary Books, 2002), p. 177.

4. Meyers-Thompson and Perkins, p. 178.

5. Mann.

6. Ibid.

7. Anna Mulrine, "Making Babies," *U.S. News & World Report,* September 27, 2004, p. 63.

8. Ibid., p. 61, and Amy Argetsinger, "Two Mothers, One Pregnancy—and Five Heartbeats," *The Milwaukee Journal Sentinel,* April 17, 2005, p. 10A.

9. Mann.

10. Ibid.

11. Ibid.

12. Ibid.

13. Ibid.

14. Ibid.

15. Ibid.

16. Ibid.

17. Meyers-Thompson and Perkins., pp. 192–193.

18. Mulrine, p. 66.

19. Mann.

20. Brigid McMenamin, "Heir at Last," *Forbes*, vol. 169, no. 4, February 18, 2002, p. 116.

21. Mann.

22. McMenamin, p. 117.

23. Telephone interview with Rachel Mann, July 29, 2004.

24. Ibid.

25. Marilyn Marchione, "Being too fat, too thin may hurt male fertility," *The Milwaukee Journal,* October 22, 2004, p. 4A.

26. Michele St. Martin, "Donor Egg & Sperm: A Family-Building Alternative for the Infertile," *Preconception.com: for those who are trying to conceive*, n.d., <www.preconception.com/resources/articles/donorprograms.htm> (May 26, 2004).

27. Ibid.

28. Telephone interview with Estril Strawn, July 3, 2004.

29. Ibid.

30. Ibid.

31. Meyers-Thompson and Perkins, p. 296.

Chapter 6 What Is Right and What Is Wrong?
Ethical Issues in High-Tech Reproduction

1. Telephone interview with Gloria Halverson, March 11, 2005.

2. Telephone interview with Robyn Shapiro, March 22, 2005.

3. Halverson.

4. Ethics Committee of the American Society for Reproductive Medicine, "Fertility Treatment When the Prognosis Is Very Poor or Futile," *Fertility and Sterility*, vol. 82, no. 4, October 2004, p. 807.

5. Ibid., p. 809.

6. Halverson.

7. Liz Sabot, "Study: Guidelines Lower Multiple Births," *USA Today*, April 15, 2004, <http://search.epnet.com/direct.asp?an= JOE302058224504&db=15h> (June 29, 2004).
8. Halverson.
9. Shapiro.
10. Ibid.
11. Debra Rosenberg, Suzanne Smalley, and Rena Kirsch, "The War Over Fetal Rights," *Newsweek*, vol.141, no. 23, June 9, 2003, p. 40.
12. Shapiro.
13. Halverson.
14. Rosenberg, Smalley, and Kirsch, p. 60.
15. David Caruso, "Fertility Clinics Vary on Embryo Disposal," *Associated Press Yahoo News*, n.d., <wysiwyg://36/http://news.yahoo.com/news?t...7/ap_on_he_me/embryo_disposal_3&printer=1> (September 17, 2004).
16. Ibid.
17. Rosenberg, p. 60.
18. Caruso.
19. Halverson.
20. Ethics Committee of the American Society of Reproductive Medicine, "Donating Spare Embryos for Embryonic Stem Cell Research," *Fertility and Sterility*, vol. 78, no. 5, November 2002, p. 959.
21. Shapiro.
22. Halverson.
23. Ethics Committee of the American Society of Reproductive Medicine, "Sex Selection and Preimplantation Genetic Diagnosis," *Fertility and Sterility*, vol. 72, no. 4, October 1999, p. 598.
24. Shapiro.
25. Jennifer Wolff, "Sperm Donor Ruling Could Open Doors for Offspring," *USA Today*, June 15, 2004, <http://search.epnet.com/direct.asp?an=JOE095044609204&db=f5h> (June 29, 2004).
26. Shapiro.

27. Ethics Committee of the American Society of Reproductive Medicine, "Financial Incentives in Recruitment of Oocyte Donors," *Fertility and Sterility*, vol. 74, no. 2, August 2000, pp. 218–219.

28. Michele St. Martin, "Donor Egg & Sperm: a Family-Building Alternative for the Infertile," *Preconception.com: for those who are trying to conceive*, n.d., <www.preconception.com/resources/articles/donorprograms.htm> (May 26, 2004).

29. Halverson.

30. St. Martin.

31. Halverson.

32. Ethics Committee of the American Society of Reproductive Medicine, "Family Members as Gamete Donors and Surrogates," *Fertility and Sterility*, vol. 80, no. 5, November 2003, p. 1129.

33. Amy Argetsinger, "Two Mothers, One Pregnancy—and Five Heartbeats," *The Milwaukee Journal Sentinel*, April 17, 2005, p. 10A.

34. Ibid.

35. Shapiro.

36. Halverson.

37. Ibid.

38. Shapiro.

39. Ethics Committee of the American Society of Reproductive Medicine, "Family Members as Gamete Donors and Surrogates," p. 1127.

40. Shapiro.

Chapter 7 Brave New World: Coming Advances in Infertility Treatment

1. Telephone interview with Rachel Mann, July 20, 2004.

2. Ibid.

3. Blythe Bernhard, "$10,000 Is Minimum Bet in Gamble on Frozen Eggs," *The Daily Item*, August 22, 2005, <http://www.dailyitem.com/archive/2005/0822/fea/stories/06fea.htm> (November 9, 2005).

4. "Woman Gets Pregnant With Donor's Frozen Eggs," *ABC News*, November 8, 2005, <http://www.abcnews.go.com/GMA/DrJohnson/story?id=1291305&CMP=OTC-RssFeeds0312> (November 9, 2005).

5. Jackie Meyers-Thompson and Sharon Perkins, *Fertility for Dummies* (New York: Wiley Publishing, 2003), p. 331.

6. Ibid., p. 243.

7. Ibid., p. 337.

Glossary

antibodies—"Watchdog" cells that attack foreign invaders in the body. They are good when they attack germs but can be harmful when they turn their attack on parts of the body or sperm.

assisted reproductive technology (ART)—The medical field that helps infertile couples to achieve pregnancy using various kinds of medications and technology.

blastocyst—An embryo that has been allowed to grow for several days, creating a ball of cells.

cannula—A tube used to place sperm or fertilized embryos into a woman's reproductive system.

conception—The joining of a male sperm and a female egg to create a genetically distinct embryo. It is also called fertilization.

condom—A latex sleeve that fits over the penis and collects the sperm, thus preventing conception.

contraceptive—A device that prevents pregnancy.

donors—People who give an infertile couple something to make pregnancy possible. There are sperm donors, egg donors, and embryo donors. Often, but not always, they are paid.

egg—The common name given to the female reproductive cell, medically called an oocyte or ovum. It carries the female DNA, which when united with the DNA in the male reproductive cell (sperm) creates a genetically unique embryo.

egg retrieval—Going into the woman's body to collect eggs from her ovaries after they have been stimulated with drugs to produce more than one egg. They are then fertilized in a petri dish to create an embryo.

ejaculation—The burst of sperm mixed with fluids called semen that comes from a man's penis when he ejaculates.

embryo—A tiny ball of cells created when the DNA in a sperm cell unites with the DNA in an egg cell. The fertilized egg divides, then divides again and again to become an embryo. The embryo is genetically distinct from the male and female cells that created it and contains the "blueprint" for the human being it will become.

embryo donation—When an infertile couple has her eggs and his sperm combined in a petri dish, often more than one embryo is formed. The "extras" are usually frozen and can be donated to another couple.

embryonic stem cell research—Using the cells from a embryo to do medical research to try to find cures for various diseases. Since the embryo is destroyed, some people think that type of research is unethical; others think it is ethical.

endometriosis—An abnormal condition in which the lining of a woman's uterus leaves that organ and attaches to other organs, such as the ovaries, in her abdomen. It may block her fallopian tubes and is a major cause of infertility.

estrogen—The primary female sex hormone.

ethics—The study of right and wrong. Assisted reproduction creates many ethical issues, and people differ on what they think is ethical or unethical.

fallopian tubes—The tubes that carry eggs from a woman's ovaries to her uterus. If they are blocked by scar tissue, infertility may result.

fertility drugs—Drugs that stimulate a woman's ovaries to start producing eggs, or to produce more than one egg per month. The most common drug is called Clomid.

fertilization—The process in which a sperm cell penetrates an egg cell. The DNA of the two cells join and the resulting cell begins to divide. The fertilized egg continues dividing until it becomes an embryo. Fertilization is also called conception.

follicle—The tissue within the ovary containing an egg.

genetic selection—Looking at a cell from an embryo to see if it carries any genetic disease and what sex it is.

hormones—The chemical messengers of the body. Hormones carry messages to many different organs to tell them how to function. Reproductive hormones stimulate the ovaries to mature and release eggs and thicken the lining of the uterus to support a growing baby. Hormones that are not in correct balance can be a cause of infertility.

infertility—Being unable to become pregnant, to carry a pregnancy to full term, or to father a child.

intrauterine insemination (IUI)—A type of artificial insemination in which a man's sperm is placed into a woman's uterus using a tube called a cannula. It is used when normal sexual intercourse is not successful at achieving a pregnancy. It may be used when the man's sperm contain antibodies or are slow "swimmers" or when donor sperm are being used.

in vitro fertilization (IVF)—Creation of an embryo outside the human body. It is done by placing a man's sperm and a woman's egg in a petri dish, allowing fertilization and several days' growth to take place, and then transferring the embryo to the woman's uterus.

laparoscopy—A procedure allowing doctors to put a lighted scope into the abdomen through tiny incisions so they can see if anything is wrong inside.

menstruation—The process by which the lining of the uterus, which has thickened to prepare for a possible pregnancy, breaks down and sheds if there is no pregnancy. Menstruation normally happens every twenty-eight days.

motility—The ability of sperm to swim. Sperm with low motility may not be able to reach the egg in time to fertilize it.

ovaries—The organs, one on each side of the uterus, that contain a woman's egg cells. One egg matures and is released each month in response to a complicated system of hormonal stimulation. If the ovaries are not producing eggs, the woman is infertile.

ovulation—The process in which the mature egg bursts free of the follicle in the ovary. If a woman does not ovulate, she is infertile.

petri dish—A flat plastic dish used in research labs for many purposes, especially to grow organisms such as bacteria or viruses. Human eggs and sperm are placed in one for fertilization to occur outside the human body.

puberty—The time at which the human body becomes capable of reproduction. The age varies from about twelve to sixteen years of age.

semen—The fluid, created in a man's prostate gland, which carries the sperm cells.

sexual intercourse—The act in which the man places his penis into a female's vagina and ejaculates sperm.

sexually transmitted disease (STD)—A disease in which the germs are spread by sexual contact. An STD can cause scar tissue, a common cause of infertility. The risk of STDs can be minimized, although not eliminated, by using condoms.

sperm—The male reproductive cells that are produced in the testes and expelled from the body through the penis. The cells carry the DNA, which, when united with the DNA in a female reproductive cell (egg), create a genetically unique embryo.

sperm count—The number of sperm in a man's ejaculation. The normal number is in the millions. A man with a low sperm count may need help to become a father.

sterile—A man who is unable to father a baby or a woman who is unable to become pregnant is called sterile. The term is not used as much today; it has been replaced by "infertile."

surrogate—A woman who carries a pregnancy for another woman who cannot do so. Most often the surrogate has an embryo created by IVF implanted in her uterus.

test-tube baby—The name some people call a child conceived by IVF. The name is not correct because a petri dish, not a test tube, is usually used for fertilization.

testosterone—The primary male sex hormone.

transfer—The process in which an embryo that was created in a petri dish in a lab is placed into the uterus of a woman.

ultrasound—A tool for diagnosing medical problems; it bounces sound waves off the body to create a picture.

uterus—The organ, located in a woman's abdomen, in which a fertilized egg implants and grows into a baby.

washed sperm—Sperm that have been spun in a centrifuge to spin off all the fluid and cells other than sperm cells. Washed sperm can be placed directly into a woman's uterus to increase the chances of conception.

workup—What doctors call a series of diagnostic tests to determine why a woman is not becoming pregnant.

For More Information

American Fertility Association

666 Fifth Avenue

New York, NY 10103

888-917-3777

Division of Reproductive Health

National Center for Chronic Disease Prevention
and Health Promotion

Centers for Disease Control

4770 Buford Highway, N.E.

Mail Stop K20

Atlanta, Ga. 30341-3717

770-488-5200

RESOLVE

1310 Broadway

Somerville, Mass. 02144-1779

617-623-0744

**InterNational Council on Infertility Information
Dissemination, Inc.**

P.O. Box 6836

Arlington, Va. 22206

703-379-9178

Further Reading

Books

Fullick, Ann. *Test Tube Babies: In Vitro Fertilization.* Chicago: Heinemann Library, 2002.

Kerrod, Robin. *Medicine: Present Knowledge, Future Trends.* North Mankato, Minn.: Smart Apple Media, 2005.

Kranz, Rachel. *Reproductive Rights and Technology.* New York: Facts on File, 2002.

Macdonald, Fiona. *The First Test Tube Baby.* Milwaukee: World Almanac Library, 2004.

Stock, Gregory. *Redesigning Humans: Choosing Our Genes, Changing Our Future.* Boston: Houghton Mifflin, 2003.

Zach, Kim. *Reproductive Technology.* San Diego: Thomson/Gale, 2004.

Internet Addresses

Infertility Page: American Society for Reproductive Medicine
    <http://www.asrm.org/Patients/topics/infertility.html>

InterNational Council on Infertility Information dissemination
    <http://www.inciid.org>

RESOLVE: The National Infertility Association
    <http://www.resolve.org>

Index